DIGITAL RICE COOKER BLISS

150 Easy Recipes for Fast, Healthy, Family-Friendly Meals

By

Chris De Sarno & Ajay Kapoor

Digital Rice Cooker Bliss: 150 Easy Recipes for Fast, Healthy, Family-Friendly Meals

Published by Rascal Face Press
www.RascalFacePress.com

Cover photo credit:
vision.si/ Depositphotos.com

Back cover: All photos from Depositphotos.com
StudioM, Anna_Shepulova, ramonespelt1, nata_vkusidey, studioM, nito103, aremafoto, elenathewise, studioM

Interior photos: All interior photos are from Depositphotos.com
kumarmukesh p. 9, Mizina p. 13, Shusha p. 15, rojoimages p. 17, okkijan p. 20, bhofack2 p. 22, rakratchada p. 23, nata_vkusidey p. 46, stevemc p. 72, nito103 p. 105, belchonock p. 116, LAMeeks p. 122, studiom p. 123, studioM p. 140, nata_vkusidey p. 168, fudio p. 170, asimojet p. 176, ramonespelt1 p. 205, lenyvavsha p. 220, gbh007 p. 224, resnick_joshua1 p. 245, Anna_Shepulova p. 253, ezumeimages p. 295, belchonock p. 299, studioM p. 302, yingko p. 307

Table of Contents

1

INTRODUCTION

Recipe Selections

This selection of rice cooker recipes includes dishes from popular cuisines from around the world. The main recipe categories that are included in this selection are from Asia, Europe, the Middle East and the US. These unique versions of rice cooker recipes are easy to prepare and require less supervision while cooking your favorite dishes at home. Cooking food with a rice cooker is also safe and healthy. It is healthy in that the nutrients in the food are retained during the cooking process.

These delicious recipes also include famous rice, breakfast, lunch and dinner recipes from around the world. You can choose from Asian recipes which include a wide variety of mouth-watering and flavorful dishes from all over Asia. The selection also includes Middle Eastern recipes that are rich in flavor and very filling. And if you want to have some light meals but still with savory and decadent tastes, try the European recipes which can be prepared easily in a rice cooker but still taste gourmet. For savory foods that satisfy your appetite, this wide recipe selection also provides the best American dishes.

Benefits of Cooking with a Rice Cooker

The Rice cooker is of course, used specifically to cook rice. But because of its unique features and convenience, more and more people use it to cook other dishes in addition to just rice. It likely has measuring cups for the right amounts of rice to use, and the corresponding water line located in the inner cooking pot for the required amount of water to ensure cooking success every time. And because it requires less supervision while cooking, it is convenient for busy people and allows you to work on other things at the same time. In addition to that, when the food is done it automatically switches to keep warm mode which makes cooking a worry-free task. It is less likely to produce burnt food on the bottom of the inner pot and provides you with fluffy and perfectly cooked rice due to its accurate rice to water ratio.

But not only that, your rice cooker is also perfect for steaming and preparing soups, stews and chili recipes. The cooking process is the same as cooking rice and is convenient, reliable and very safe. You can use it to cook a complete dinner with side dishes, main dishes and even desserts. With a good rice cooker in your kitchen, you can also save money by buying rice in bulk.

Advantages of a Rice Cooker

With the unique features of most rice cookers, cooking your favorite rice recipes and dishes is easy and effortless due to the programmable digital controls. You'll also often have brown and white rice functions for you to prepare varieties of rice recipes.

And because of its' non-stick inner cooking pot, cleaning the appliance is very easy. There is often a delay timer feature which allows cooking dishes to be ready at the specific time when they are to be served. You can use this feature by setting the wanted number of hours for the food to be cooked and just leave it and come back when the dish is done. Cook rice or any other dish in the inner cooking pot and steam or reheat foods on the steam tray simultaneously.

2

How to Use a Rice Cooker

Basic Operations for Digital Controls

Delay Timer

A DELAY TIMER BUTTON is used for preparing dishes ahead of time according to the number of hours or the time wanted for it to be served. You can set the delay timer and come back when it is done and serve it right away, perfectly cooked.

White Rice Button

Some models will have a WHITE RICE BUTTON which is specifically used for all white rice varieties from short, medium, and long-grain types of rice that are perfectly cooked to restaurant-quality but prepared so easily.

Brown Rice Button

The BROWN RICE BUTTON is (you guessed it!) used for brown rice varieties which are very starchy making them tough-to-cook ordinarily. But with this unique feature and together with the delay timer, soaking brown rice is omitted by setting the delay timer with the equivalent amount of time for soaking brown rice ingredients.

Steam

The STEAM BUTTON is used for preparing steamed vegetables and other side dishes perfectly without worrying about overcooked foods because it automatically shuts off after the programmed steaming time has elapsed.

Keep-Warm

The KEEP-WARM BUTTON is used to maintain before serving dishes. It is also very useful because it is automatically switched when the food is done which results in less burnt food on the bottom of the inner cooking pot and keeps the cooked food warm for up to 10 hours.

How to Cook Rice

1. Using the provided measuring cup, take the amount of rice needed and place it in a fine strainer.
2. Rinse with cool running water and drain thoroughly.
3. Transfer the rice into the inner cooking pot.
4. Fill the inner cooking pot with the corresponding amount of water using the line located on the inner pot.
5. Place the inner cooking pot into the rice cooker and stir to combine.
6. Close the lid securely.
7. Turn on the rice cooker by pressing the power button, and then press the white rice or brown rice button to start cooking.
8. The cooking indicator light of the rice cooker will illuminate and display a chasing pattern when the cooking process has started.
9. The digital display of the rice cooker will show a 12 minute final countdown before the rice is fully cooked.

10. When the rice is done, the rice cooker will produce a beep sound and automatically switches to keep warm mode. The rice should remain in keep warm mode no longer than 10 hours.

11. Before serving, fluff the rice with the serving spatula and serve warm.

How to Use the Delay Timer

1. Each press of the delay timer is equivalent to one hour intervals. The delay timer of the rice cooker can be set from 1 up to 15 hours.
2. When the required time has been set, press the white or brown rice button depending on the variety of rice used.
3. The digital display of the rice cooker will show a countdown of the expected time when the rice is cooked.
4. The cooking indicator light of the rice cooker will illuminate and display a cashing pattern when the cooking process has started.
5. The digital display of the rice cooker will show a 12 minute final countdown before the rice is fully cooked.
6. When the rice is done, the rice cooker will produce a beep sound and automatically switch to keep warm mode. Limit the time in keep warm mode to 10 hours or less.
7. Before serving, fluff the rice with the serving spatula and serve warm.

How to Steam

1. Using the provided measuring cup, add the required amount of water according to the type of ingredient to steam in the inner cooking pot.
2. Locate the steam tray over the inner cooking pot and add the ingredient to steam on the tray.

3. Transfer the inner cooking pot into the rice cooker and close the lid securely.
4. Turn on the rice cooker by pressing the power button and then press the steam button. It will indicate 5 minutes initially and the

next press will set 1 minute intervals. Set to the required steaming time to start cooking and after the time has been set the rice cooker will produce a beep sound to indicate that the steaming process has started.

5. When the water reaches a boil, the cooking indicator light of the rice cooker will illuminate and display a chasing pattern when the steaming process has started.

6. The digital display of the rice cooker will show 1 minute intervals from the time selected for steaming.

7. When the time selected has passed, the rice cooker will beep and automatically switches to keep warm mode.

8. To avoid over cooking, remove the steam tray carefully and transfer to a bowl with an ice bath to stop further cooking.

How to Cook Soups, Stews and Chili

1. Place all ingredients of the recipe into the inner cooking pot.
2. Transfer the inner cooking pot into the rice cooker.
3. Stir briefly and close the lid securely.
4. Plug the power cord into the electric source and turn on the rice cooker by pressing the power button to start cooking.
5. The cooking indicator light of the rice cooker will illuminate and will show a chasing pattern when the cooking process has started.
6. Use a wooden spoon with a long handle to stir the ingredients to avoid burning on the bottom of the inner cooking pot.
7. When the dish is done and cooking process is complete, switch to keep-warm mode to stop the cooking process and keep the food warm before serving.

Rice Cooker Tips

1. When using a rice cooker for cooking, it is recommended to lightly spray or coat the inner cooking pot with oil for easier clean-up and less food stuck to the bottom.
2. When the rice cooker has switched to keep warm mode and the rice or dish is not yet done, add more water if needed and reset the rice cooker to cook again. Manually switch to keep warm mode when the food is done.
3. For added flavor and aroma, use equal amounts of stock or broth to substitute for the water.

4. You can also add herbs and spices in cooking rice for extra aroma. Just place the herbs and spices in a spice sachet or wrap it in cheesecloth. Discard the spice sachet when the cooking process is finished.
5. In steaming foods with a rice cooker, use extreme caution when lifting the lid to avoid steam burns and injuries from the high temperature of steam coming out of the rice cooker. Keep your hands and face away from the rice cooker when opening the lid.
6. Use a cloth in removing the inner cooking pot from the rice cooker after cooking.
7. Use a tong and wooden spoon with a long handle in cooking dishes to avoid injuries and burns from the hot surface of the rice cooker.
8. The provided serving spatula is only for serving and fluffing the rice, do not use this in stirring and sautéing ingredients.
9. Do not place the inner pot into the rice cooker if the bottom is wet. It may damage the unit and may cause electrical problems and fire.

Rice Cooker Cleaning Tips

1. Unplug the rice cooker after cooking and make sure that the unit is completely cool before washing.
2. Remove the inner cooking pot, steam tray and other accessories from the rice cooker and wash with warm water and soap.
3. Only use a sponge or dishcloth in washing the accessories, wipe the washed accessories and all parts of the rice cooker with dry cloth.
4. Remove the condensation collector and discard the liquid, and also remove the steam vent. Wipe with dry cloth and remember to reattach before using the rice cooker again.

RICE

Basic White Rice

There are very few meals that won't work with white rice as a base. A solid recipe for white rice is indispensable for any cook, so keep this one close – you'll be using it often!

Recipe for 8 Cup Rice Cooker and Food Steamer

Cooking time: 28 to 37 minutes

Yields: 4 to 6 cups

INGREDIENTS:

2 cups of Basmati rice or any long-grain rice, rinsed and drained

Water, as needed to fill up to line 2

Salt, to taste (optional)

Fresh parsley, chopped for garnish (optional)

DIRECTIONS:

1. Using the provided measuring cup, take 2 cups of rice and place it in a fine strainer. Rinse with cool running water and drain thoroughly. Transfer rice to the inner cooking pot.
2. Fill the inner cooking pot with water up to line 2. Place the inner cooking pot into the rice cooker, swirl to combine and close the lid securely.
3. Press the power button to turn on the rice cooker, and then press the white rice button to start cooking.
4. When the rice is done, the rice cooker will produce a beep sound and automatically switches to keep warm mode. Let it sit for 10 minutes.
5. Fluff the rice and transfer into serving bowls or plates. Serve warm.

White Rice Pilaf, Jasmine Rice

This classic rice dish is a traditional favorite in much of the world for good reason. There's nothing quite like the aroma of jasmine mingling with the nuts, mushrooms and chicken stock in this recipe. Best of all, this is a vitamin-rich preparation, ensuring your rice will be as nutritious as it is delicious!

Recipe for 8-cup Rice Cooker and Food Steamer

Cooking time: 28 to 37 minutes

Yields: 4 to 6 cups

INGREDIENTS:

2 cups Jasmine rice, rinsed and drained

chicken stock, as needed to fill up to line 2

¼ cup chopped almonds

½ cup button mushrooms, halved

1 shallot, minced

½ tablespoon butter or olive oil

1 garlic clove, minced

DIRECTIONS:

1. Using the provided measuring cup, take 2 cups of rice and place it in a fine strainer. Rinse with cool running water and drain thoroughly. Transfer rice into the inner cooking pot. Set aside.
2. In a pan over medium heat, melt in the butter and add the garlic and shallots. Cook for 2 minutes or until lightly brown and aromatic, and stir in the mushrooms. Cook for another 1 minute and remove from heat.

3. Stir the sautéed ingredients and chopped almonds into the inner cooking pot with the rice. Fill the inner cooking pot with chicken stock up to line 2. Place the inner cooking pot into the rice cooker, swirl to combine and close the lid securely.
4. Press the power button to turn on the rice cooker, and then press the white rice button to start cooking.
5. When the rice is done, the rice cooker will produce a beep sound and automatically switches to keep warm mode. Let it sit for 10 minutes.
6. Fluff the rice and transfer into serving bowls or plates. Serve warm.

NOTE:

Do not exceed 10 hours in keep warm mode.

BASIC BROWN RICE

I'm calling this dish "basic" because it is such an all-purpose staple – but the truth is there's nothing basic about a well-cooked bowl of nutritious brown rice. This is the perfect rice to make a substantial meal of any meat or vegetable recipe, and an excellent way to showcase your favorite sauce.

Recipe for 8-cup Rice Cooker and Food Steamer

Cooking time: 65 to 75 minutes

Yields: 4 to 6 cups

INGREDIENTS:

2 cups of brown rice (long, medium or short-grain rice), rinsed and drained

Water or chicken stock, as needed to fill up to line 2

Butter or oil, for greasing

Salt, to taste (optional)

DIRECTIONS:

1. Using the provided measuring cup, take 2 cups of brown rice and place it in a fine strainer. Rinse with cool running water and drain thoroughly. Transfer rice into the inner cooking pot. Season to taste with salt if preferred.
2. Fill the inner cooking pot with water or stock up to line 2. Place the inner cooking pot into the rice cooker, swirl to combine and close the lid securely.
3. Press the power button to turn on the rice cooker, and then press the brown rice button to start cooking.
4. When the rice is done, the rice cooker will produce a beep sound and automatically switches to keep warm mode. Let it sit for 10 minutes.

5. Fluff the rice and transfer into serving bowls or plates. Serve warm.

NOTE:

If your rice is too dry when the rice cooker switches to keep warm mode, adjust by adding water as needed depending on the texture of cooked rice. Cook further until it switches to keep warm mode, or until the rice is soft and moist.

If your rice is too moist or soggy when the rice cooker switches to keep warm mode, fluff the rice with the serving spatula and close the lid. Maintain keep warm mode for 10 to 30 minutes, or as needed until the rice is cooked through. Fluff rice occasionally to release excess moisture.
Do not exceed 10 hours in keep warm mode.

Red Rice

Red rice gets its special color from the flavonoids in the grains, which makes it not only gorgeous to look at, but incredibly healthy to consume. The light nutty flavor in this rice is the perfect complement to any hot dish – and your dining table will look extra-pretty for it!

Recipe for 8-cup Rice Cooker and Food Steamer

Cooking time: 65 to 75 minutes

Yields: 4 to 6 cups

INGREDIENTS:

2 cups of red rice, rinsed and drained

Water or chicken stock, as needed to fill up to line 2

Butter or oil, for greasing

Salt, to taste (optional)

DIRECTIONS:

1. Lightly grease the inner cooking pot with oil or butter. Set aside.
2. Using the provided measuring cup, take 2 cups of red rice and place in a fine strainer. Rinse with cool running water and drain thoroughly. Transfer rice into the inner cooking pot. Season to taste with salt if preferred.
3. Fill the inner cooking pot with water up to line 2. Place the inner cooking pot into the rice cooker, swirl to combine and close the lid securely.
4. Press the power button to turn on the rice cooker, and then press the brown rice button to start cooking.

5. When the rice is done, the rice cooker will produce a beep sound and automatically switches to keep warm mode. Let it sit for 10 minutes.
6. Fluff the rice and transfer into serving bowls or plates. Serve warm.

NOTE:

If your rice is too dry when the rice cooker switches to keep warm mode, adjust by adding water as needed depending on the texture of cooked rice. And cook further until it switches to keep warm mode, or until the rice is soft and moist.

If your rice is too moist or soggy when the rice cooker switches to keep warm mode, fluff the rice with the serving spatula and close the lid. Maintain keep warm mode for 10 to 30 minutes, or as needed until the rice is cooked through. Fluff rice occasionally to release excess moisture.

Do not exceed 10 hours in keep warm mode.

Wild Rice

Wild rice is not just an extra-healthy long-grain with complex nutrients – it's also the fastest and easiest way to take a meal from mundane to marvelous! The multicolored grains and earthy textures of this rice the perfect base for stews, ragouts, or simply the sauce and vegetables of your choice.

Recipe for 8-cup Rice Cooker and Food Steamer

Cooking time: 65 to 75 minutes

Yields: 4 to 6 cups

INGREDIENTS:

2 cups of wild rice, rinsed and drained

Water or chicken stock, as needed to fill up to line 2

Butter or oil, for greasing

Salt, to taste (optional)

DIRECTIONS:

1. Lightly grease the inner cooking pot with oil or butter. Set aside.
2. Using the provided measuring cup, take 2 cups of wild rice and place it in a fine strainer. Rinse with cool running water and drain thoroughly. Transfer rice into the inner cooking pot. Season to taste with salt if desired.
3. Fill the inner cooking pot with water up to line 2. Place the inner cooking pot into the rice cooker, swirl to combine and close the lid securely.
4. Set the delay timer for when the rice is needed to be served.
5. Press the power button to turn on the rice cooker, and then press the brown rice button to start cooking.

6. When the rice is done, the rice cooker will produce a beep sound and automatically switches to keep warm mode. Let it stand for 10 minutes.
7. Fluff the rice and transfer into serving bowls or plates. Serve warm.

NOTE:

If your rice is too dry when the rice cooker switches to keep warm mode, adjust by adding water as needed depending on the texture of cooked rice. And cook further until it switches to keep warm mode, or until the rice is soft and moist.

If your rice is too moist or soggy when the rice cooker switches to keep warm mode, fluff the rice with the serving spatula and close the lid. Maintain keep warm mode for 10 to 30 minutes, or as needed until the rice is cooked through. Fluff rice occasionally to release excess moisture.

Do not exceed 10 hours in keep warm mode.

Chinese Style Fried Rice

This take-out food staple is hugely popular in my house – but the truth is, everyone loves it best when I make it in my very own kitchen. With fresh seasonings and meats, and so much less grease than is typical in take-out fare, this rice is a feast unto itself!

Recipe for 8-cup Rice Cooker and Food Steamer

Cooking time: 45 minutes

Yields: 4 to 6 cups

INGREDIENTS:

2 medium onions, diced

1 garlic clove, minced

2 to 3 tablespoons olive oil

2 whole eggs, beaten

1 teaspoon light soy sauce

1 teaspoon fish sauce

½ tablespoon of sesame oil

1 cup cooked pork meat or chicken breast, deboned and cut into strips

1 medium carrot, peeled and diced

½ cup canned peas, drained

2 cups white rice, rinsed and drained

Chicken stock, as needed to fill up

2 spring onions, chopped

1 cup mung bean sprouts, rinsed and drained

Salt and pepper, to taste

DIRECTIONS:

1. Place the inner cooking pot in the rice cooker and turn on the rice cooker. Press the white rice button to begin cooking and add 1 tablespoon of oil. Once the oil is hot, add in the diced onions and sauté until lightly brown and fragrant while stirring occasionally. Stir in the garlic and sauté for another minute, or until brown and fragrant. Remove from inner pot and set aside.
2. Whisk together the beaten eggs, fish sauce and light soy sauce, pour into the inner cooking pot and cook until lightly brown. Flip the egg and cook for another minute. Remove from inner pot, set aside to cool and chop into pieces.
3. Add 1 tablespoon of oil and add in the meat. Cook for 1 minute and stir in the sautéed onions and garlic, peas and carrots. Stir occasionally and cook for 2 minutes. Remove from the inner cooking pot and set aside. Add the rinsed and drained rice into the inner pot.
4. Fill the inner cooking pot with stock up to line 2. Stir briefly, close the lid and press the white rice button to cook. When the rice is done and in keep warm mode, open lid and fluff the rice. Stir in the cooked ingredients, together with the sesame oil, spring onions and bean sprouts. Stir until well combined and season to taste with salt and pepper. Maintain keep warm mode for 10 minutes while stirring occasionally.
5. Transfer fried rice to serving bowls or plates and serve warm with extra spring onions on top if desired.

Thai Fried Rice with Prawns and Peas

This rice dish is a sumptuous entrée all by itself, and a perfectly balanced meal at that. With the lean protein of fresh prawns, nutritious green peas, and the perfect combination of spices and seasonings, this is the kind of rice dish you'll find yourself preparing on a regular basis – to rave reviews from your friends, family, and guests.

Recipe for 8-cup Rice Cooker and Food Steamer

Cooking time: 40 to 45 minutes

Yields: 4 to 6 cups

INGREDIENTS:

2 tablespoons of oil

1 medium onion, halved and thinly sliced

2 garlic cloves, minced

1 red hot chili, chopped

1 cup raw prawns, peeled and deveined

2 cups brown rice, soaked and drained

Water, as needed to fill up to line 2

½ cup canned peas, drained

1 tablespoon light soy sauce

1 tablespoon fish sauce

½ cup loosely packed fresh coriander, chopped

4 large whole eggs, beaten

Hot chili sauce, as needed for extra heat (optional)

DIRECTIONS:

1. Drain the soaked brown rice a couple of hours before cooking the Thai Fried Rice. Place into the inner pot and fill with water up to line 2. Place the inner pot in the rice cooker, turn on and press brown rice button to start cooking. Set delay timer for when the rice is needed to be served. Once the rice is ready, turn off cooker and fluff with serving spatula. Transfer to a bowl or plate and set aside.
2. Wash the inner cooking pot and wipe with cloth. Place it into the rice cooker, turn on and press brown rice button to start cooking the fried rice recipe. Add a tablespoon of oil and add in the beaten egg, cook until lightly brown and flip to cook the other side for another minute. Remove from the inner pot, set aside to cool and chop into small pieces.
3. Pour in 1 tablespoon of oil and add in the onion, garlic and chili and sauté until soft and fragrant, for about 2 minutes. Add the prawns and cook until opaque in color then stir in the peas and rice. Season to taste with salt and pepper if desired, stir in ¾ of the coriander and cook for about 3 minutes while stirring occasionally. Remove from the inner cooking pot.
4. Portion fried rice into individual serving bowls. Serve with the eggs, onion mix and prawns. Top with coriander and chili sauce if desired.

BENIHANA JAPANESE FRIED RICE

This rice was popularized in America by the Japanese food-chain Benihana, but you don't have to go out to enjoy this awesome dish right at home. This recipe also packs a full serving of veggies, so rest assured that you'll not only be serving up a scrumptious meal – but a healthy one, too!

Recipe for 8-cup Rice Cooker and Food Steamer

Cooking time: 40 to 45 minutes

Yields: 4 to 6 cups

INGREDIENTS:

2 cups of white long-grain rice, rinsed and drained

Water or chicken stock, as needed to fill up to line 2

1 cup canned peas, drained

1 small carrot, peeled and diced

2 whole eggs, lightly beaten

2 medium onions, diced

2 tablespoons of butter

2 tablespoons light soy sauce

Salt and pepper, to taste

DIRECTIONS:

1. Rinse and drain the rice and place into the inner cooking pot. Fill with water or stock up to line 2 and place inner pot in the rice cooker. Season to taste with salt and pepper, if desired. Turn on rice cooker and press the white rice button to start cooking. Once the rice is done, fluff with a serving spatula, transfer to a large bowl and set aside.

2. Wash the inner cooking pot and wipe with cloth. Return to the rice cooker, turn on and press the white rice button to start cooking. Add 1 tablespoon of butter to the pot. When butter has melted, fry the eggs. Use a spatula or wooden spoon to chop eggs into smaller pieces when fried. Remove from pot.
3. Melt the remaining butter in the inner pot and stir in the onions, carrots and peas. Cook for 5 minutes while stirring regularly or until the peas and carrots and tender and cooked through.
4. Stir together with the vegetables the rice, eggs, lights soy sauce and season to taste with salt and pepper. Cook for another 2 minutes and stir the ingredients until well combined. Remove the inner cooking pot from the rice cooker.
5. Portion fried rice into individual serving bowls or plates and serve warm with extra soy sauce in a separate bowl.

Lebanese Lentil/Rice Pilaf with Blackened Onions

I got this recipe from an old friend in Beirut, and it has served me wonderfully over the years. This richly spiced rice pilaf with a healthy dose of veggies is the perfect accompaniment to most any grilled or barbecued meal.

Recipe for 8-cup Rice Cooker and Food Steamer

Cooking time: 40 to 45 minutes

Yields: 4 to 6 cups

INGREDIENTS:

3 tablespoons of olive oil, divided

1 large purple onion, diced

2 garlic cloves, minced

½ tablespoon cumin powder

½ teaspoon cinnamon powder

½ teaspoon allspice mix

Vegetable broth or chicken stock, as needed to fill up to line 2

½ cup dried lentils, rinsed and drained

2 cups long-grain white rice

2 purple onions, halved and thinly sliced

3 ripe tomatoes, quartered and seeded

1 cucumber, peeled and sliced into thin rounds

Plain yogurt, for serving

Fresh mint leaves, for garnish

DIRECTIONS:

1. Rinse and drain the rice, place into a bowl set aside.
2. Place the inner cooking pot in the rice cooker, turn on and press the white rice button to start cooking. Add and heat half of the oil, add the thinly sliced onions and cook until caramelized and starting to darken in color, for about 15 to 20 minutes. Remove from the inner cooking pot and set aside.
3. Wash and clean the inner cooking pot, and the wipe with cloth. Return the inner cooking pot into the rice cooker, turn on and press the white rice button to start cooking. Add half of the oil and sauté in the garlic, diced onions, cinnamon spice, allspice mix and cumin powder. Pour in 1 cup of broth or stock and add the lentils, close the lid and bring to a boil. Stir in the rice and add more broth or stock up to line 2, close lid and wait until the rice is cooked through. When the rice is done, season to taste with salt and pepper. Fluff with a serving spatula and maintain keep warm mode for 10 minutes.
4. Portion into individual serving plates, top with blackened onions and mint leaves. Serve warm with sliced tomatoes and cucumbers on the sides, and yogurt on top, or in a separate bowl.

Gingered Chicken Rice

This recipe is truly a treat for your taste-buds. The combination of lightly spiced coconut milk, jasmine rice, fresh ginger a dose of veggies, are the perfect offset to well-cooked chicken. This recipe is a huge hit at my house, and I know your friends, family and guests will love it too.

Recipe for 8-cup Rice Cooker and Food Steamer

Cooking time: 40 to 45 minutes

Yields: 4 to 6 cups

INGREDIENTS:

1 tablespoon of ghee or oil

Water or chicken stock, as needed to fill up to line 2

2 cups of Jasmine rice, rinsed and drained

2 chicken thighs, skinned and deboned, cubed into 1-inch pieces

2 pieces of 1-inch fresh ginger root, peeled and cut into juliennes

2 cups tightly packed baby spinach, rinsed

1 cup of fresh coconut milk, or canned if unavailable

Salt and pepper, to taste

Fresh parsley leaves, chopped for garnish

DIRECTIONS:

1. Rinse and drain the rice, place into a bowl and set aside. Skin and debone chicken, cut into cubes and season with salt and pepper.
2. Place the inner cooking pot in the rice cooker, turn on and press the white rice button to start cooking. Add the ghee and fry the chicken until brown while stirring occasionally. Turn off the rice cooker and remove meat from the inner cooking pot, transfer to a bowl and set aside.

3. Place the drained rice, ginger and chicken in the inner cooking pot and place it in the rice cooker. Pour in the coconut milk and fill with stock up to line 2. Place and arrange the baby spinach on top, season to taste with salt and pepper and close the lid. Turn on the rice cooker and press the white rice button to start cooking.

4. When the rice is done, fluff with a serving spatula and check for doneness. If the rice is too moist, fluff and press the white rice button to cook further until it switches to keep warm mode. If the rice is too dry, add ½ cup of liquid and fluff the rice. Close the lid and maintain keep warm mode until the rice is soft. Let it rest for 10 minutes.

5. Portion into individual serving bowls, serve warm with chopped parsley on top.

Middle Eastern Rice with Black Beans and Chickpeas

This awesome rice loaded with nutrient-rich beans and chickpeas is a wonderful health-conscious entrée. The cilantro in the spice mix gives the whole dish a refreshing zing, while the pepper and clove ensure that every bite carries a delicious kick.

Recipe for 8-cup Rice Cooker and Food Steamer

Cooking time: 40 to 45 minutes

Yields: 4 to 6 cups

INGREDIENTS:

1 tablespoon of ghee or oil

1 garlic clove, minced

2 cups Basmati rice, rinsed and drained

½ tablespoon cumin powder

½ tablespoon coriander powder

½ tablespoon turmeric powder

½ tablespoon cayenne pepper

Chicken stock, as needed to fill up to line 2

2 cups of ground turkey

2 cups canned chickpeas, drained

2 cups canned black beans, drained

1 cup loosely packed fresh cilantro, chopped (optional)

1 cup loosely packed fresh parsley leaves, chopped (optional)

¼ cup of toasted pine nuts (optional)

Salt and freshly ground black pepper, to taste

DIRECTIONS:

1. Rinse and drain the rice, place into the inner cooking pot and fill with stock up to line 2. Place the inner pot in the rice cooker, turn on and press the white rice button to start cooking. When the rice is done, fluff with a serving spatula and maintain keep warm mode for 10 minutes. Remove from the inner pot and place into a bowl, set aside.
2. Wash and clean the inner cooking pot and wipe with cloth. Return inner pot in the rice cooker, turn on and press the white rice button to start cooking. Add the ghee or oil, add and sauté the garlic until brown and aromatic. Stir in the cumin, cayenne, turmeric, coriander, ground turkey and season to taste with salt and pepper. Cook until the ground turkey is browned and most of the liquid has evaporated. Stir in the black beans, chickpeas, cilantro, parsley, pine nuts and the cooked rice. Pour in ½ cup of stock and briefly stir the ingredients, close lid and wait until the rice is warmed. Fluff rice with serving spatula, maintain keep warm mode for 10 minutes.
3. Portion into individual serving bowls or plates and serve warm with extra toasted pine nuts and parsley on top.

Saffron Rice

There's nothing quite like the exotic flavor of saffron to elevate a meal, and this finely flavored basmati rice with saffron and raisins is truly a unique treat. This rice goes wonderfully with lamb, grilled spring legumes, or any other meat or vegetable dish that could use a sophisticated savory twist.

Recipe for 8-cup Rice Cooker and Food Steamer

Cooking time: 40 to 45 minutes

Yields: 4 to 6 cups

INGREDIENTS:

¼ cup of toasted pine nuts

Water, as needed to fill up to line 2

4 to 6 saffron threads, soaked in 2 cups of warm water for 10 minutes

2 cups Basmati rice, rinsed and drained

½ cup seedless raisins

DIRECTIONS:

1. Rinse and drain rice, place in a bowl and set aside. Soak saffron threads in a bowl with warm water for 10 minutes.
2. Place the inner cooking pot in the rice cooker, turn on and press the white rice button to start cooking. Add the pine nuts and cook until lightly toasted and fragrant stirring frequently. Remove from the inner pot and transfer to a bowl, set aside.
3. Add rice to the inner cooking pot, pour in the saffron and soaking liquid. Add more water to fill the inner cooking pot up to line 2, if needed. Close the lid and press the white rice button.
4. When the rice is done, fluff with a serving spatula and maintain in keep warm mode for 10 minutes.

5. Stir in the toasted pine nuts and raisins, fluff again and portion saffron rice into individual serving bowls or plates. Serve warm.

Chicken Machboos

This succulent chicken and rice dish – which literally translates to "spiced chicken and rice" – is the national dish of Bahrain, and it's not hard to see why. The turmeric, jalapeno and onions provide a powerful flavor combination that perfectly complements the chicken, while the garlic, ginger, cardamom and lime lend an exotic and refreshing feel to the overall dish. Serve with pride – and get ready for rave reviews!

Recipe for 8-cup Rice Cooker and Food Steamer

Cooking time: 40 to 45 minutes

Yields: 4 to 6 cups

INGREDIENTS:

2 medium purple onions, diced

2 tablespoons clarified butter or ghee

2 to 3 teaspoons Baharat spice mix

½ tablespoon ground turmeric

2 tablespoons oil

2 chicken thighs

2 chicken legs

1 jalapeno, seeded and diced

1-inch fresh ginger root, minced

5 garlic cloves, crushed and sliced

1 cup canned stewed tomatoes, drained

2 Loomi or dried limes, punctured

4 pods of green cardamom

½ teaspoon cloves, ground

1 cinnamon stick

1 tablespoon salt

3 cups of Chicken stock, or as needed to fill up to line 2

2 cups Basmati rice, rinsed and drained

½ cup loosely packed fresh cilantro, roughly chopped

¼ cup loosely packed fresh parsley, roughly chopped

Rosewater for sprinkling, for serving (optional)

DIRECTIONS:

1. Rinse and drain the rice and place it in a bowl, set aside. Season chicken with salt and pepper.
2. Place the inner cooking pot in the rice cooker, turn on and press the white rice button to start cooking. Add oil and place and arrange the chicken pieces in the inner pot and cook until brown and crispy, turn and cook the other side of the chicken pieces. Remove the browned chicken from the inner pot with a tong, transfer to a plate and set aside.
3. Add the clarified butter to the inner cooking pot, and cook the onions until brown. Stir in the garlic, ginger, jalapeno and sauté until soft and fragrant. Add the Baharat spice mix and ground turmeric, cook for 1 minute while stirring occasionally.
4. Bring the browned chicken to the inner cooking pot, together with the drained tomatoes, Loomi, ground cloves, cinnamon and cardamom pods. Stir in the parsley and cilantro and pour in the stock. Season to taste with salt and pepper and cook for 1 hour. Remove the chicken and transfer to a plate, set aside. Transfer the cooking liquid to a large bowl or pot, set aside.
5. Return the inner cooking pot to the rice cooker, add the drained rice and pour in the reserved cooking liquid until it reaches to line 2. Close lid and cook until the rice is cooked through. Once the rice is done, check doneness and adjust texture by add more cooking liquid if the rice is too dry or cook further if the rice is too moist.

Dolmades (Stuffed Grape Leaves)

A staple appetizer throughout the Middle East and the Mediterranean, stuffed grape leaves are the perfect hors d'oeuvre or side-dish for any dinner party or family gathering. My recipe here uses a touch of fresh dill in the rice, which I find helps bring out the flavor of the pine nuts and the grape leaves themselves. Feel free to adjust the seasoning ratios as desired – this is my own personal favorite blend!

Recipe for 8-cup Rice Cooker and Food Steamer

Cooking time: 40 to 45 minutes

Yields: 4 to 6 cups

INGREDIENTS:

½ cup olive oil

1 large white onion, diced

1 fennel bulb, cored, halved and diced

1 teaspoon organic lemon zest

½ cup toasted pine nuts

2 cups long-grain white rice, rinsed and drained

Chicken stock, as needed to fill up to line 2

¼ cup loosely packed fresh dill leaves, chopped

¼ cup loosely packed fresh flat-leaf parsley, chopped

Salt and coarsely ground black pepper, to taste

1 cup of grape leaves, rinsed and drained

2 organic lemons, juiced

DIRECTIONS:

1. To prepare the stuffing mixture: Place the inner cooking pot in the rice cooker, turn on and press the white rice button to start cooking. Pour in half of the oil and add the onions, fennel and lemon zest and cook while stirring regularly until soft and fragrant. Stir in the pine nuts and drained rice, sauté for 2 minutes and stir ingredients to coat with the oil. Pour in the chicken stock until it reaches line 2, close lid and wait until all of the liquid has been absorbed by the rice. Fluff the rice and stir in the chopped parsley and dill, season to taste with salt and pepper. Transfer to a large bowl and set aside.
2. Wash and clean the inner cooking pot and wipe with dry cloth. Return to the rice cooker, turn on and press the white rice button to start cooking. Add 2 cups of water or stock, close lid and bring to a boil. Place the grape leaves on the steam tray and place it over the boiling stock, steam grape leaves for 5 minutes or until pliable. Remove steam tray from the rice cooker, and switch to keep warm mode.
3. Pat grape leaves dry with paper towels and lay each leaf on the work surface, shiny-side down. Add approximately 2 tablespoons of the rice stuffing, depending in the size of leaf for easy rolling. Fold the edges toward the center and roll it upwards. You can also insert a toothpick to secure the stuffed grape rolls. Repeat the process with the remaining ingredients.
4. Place the Dolmades in the inner cooking pot, seam-side down and add in the remaining oil and lemon juice. Arrange and make an even first layer of Dolmades and then place a second layer on top, and so on. You may need to add more water to cover all of the Dolmades. Press the white rice button to start cooking, and cook until the rice are cooked through and tender.
5. Carefully remove the stuffed grape leaves and transfer into a serving platter. Serve warm.

MIDDLE EASTERN RICE (MEJARDA)

The complex spice and seasoning combination in this rice makes it a memorable addition to any meal. I love the way the cinnamon counterbalances the cumin in this recipe, and how just a touch of sugar perfectly offset the shallots and pepper spicing the lentils. This dish can be a filling meal all on its own, or paired with the meat or veggies of your choice.

Recipe for 8-cup Rice Cooker and Food Steamer

Cooking time: 40 to 45 minutes

Yields: 4 to 6 cups

INGREDIENTS:

2 tablespoons ghee or oil

½ tablespoons cumin seeds

1 tablespoon coriander seeds

2 cups Basmati rice, rinsed and drained (or any long grain variety)

Water or vegetable stock, as needed to fill up to line 2

1 cup canned lentils, drained

½ teaspoon turmeric powder

½ tablespoon cinnamon powder

½ tablespoon sugar

½ teaspoon salt, to taste

Black pepper, freshly ground to taste

½ cup fried shallots

DIRECTIONS:

1. Rinse and drain rice, place it in a bowl and set aside.
2. Place the inner cooking pot in the rice cooker, turn on and press the white rice button to start cooking. Add and heat the ghee, add coriander and cumin seeds and cook until lightly toasted and fragrant. Stir in the drained rice and toss ingredients to coat rice with oil and spices.
3. Stir in the lentils and fill with water or vegetable stock up to line 2. Add the remaining ingredients except for the fried shallots, and season to taste with salt and pepper. Close lid and wait until the rice is cooked and switches to keep warm mode.
4. When the rice is done, fluff with a serving spatula and adjust seasoning if needed. Maintain keep warm mode for 10 minutes.
5. Toss in the fried shallots just before serving, portion into individual serving bowls or plates. Serve with extra fried shallots on top and yogurt.

Arroz Con Pollo

This classic Spanish chicken and rice dish is surprisingly easy to prepare at home – even if you've never been anywhere near the Iberian Peninsula! Loaded with peppers, garlic, and onion, with a chicken-stock, tomato-paste and white-wine base, this recipe infuses rich flavors throughout the chicken and rice for a truly irresistible flavor in every bite.

Recipe for 8-cup Rice Cooker and Food Steamer

Cooking time: 40 to 45 minutes

Yields: 4 to 6 cups

INGREDIENTS:

1 whole chicken, cut into 8 parts, skinned if preferred

Salt and ground black pepper, to taste

2 tablespoons of oil

2 to 3 tablespoons of tomato paste

1 green bell pepper, seeded and diced

1 onion, diced

3 garlic cloves, minced

2 red tomatoes, diced

Chicken stock, as needed to fill up to line 2

4 tablespoons of dry white wine

2 bay leaves

4 to 6 saffron threads, soaked in 1 cup warm water (optional)

2 cups of white rice, rinsed and drained

½ pound of asparagus spears, blanched and drained (optional)

½ cup canned peas, drained (optional)

1 cherry pepper or pimiento, seeded and diced (optional)

DIRECTIONS:

1. Rinse and drain the rice and place in a bowl, set aside.
2. Season chicken pieces with salt and freshly ground black pepper, rubbing all areas with hands to evenly distribute the flavoring ingredients. Place the inner cooking pot in the rice cooker, turn on and press the white rice button to start cooking. Add the oil and brown the chicken on all sides; you may need to cook them by batch so as not to overcrowd the inner pot. Turn the chicken pieces to cook the other side, add in the tomato paste and stir to evenly coat the chicken. Remove chicken from the inner cooking pot, place in a bowl and set aside.
3. Add the onions, garlic and green pepper in the inner cooking pot and cook until soft and fragrant. Stir in the rice, diced tomatoes, bay leaves, wine, soaked saffron with liquid, 1 cup of stock and season to taste with salt and freshly ground black pepper to taste. Add more stock to fill the inner cooking pot up to line 2, place the chicken pieces in the inner cooking pot.
4. Close lid and wait until the rice is cooked through and it switches to keep warm mode. Once the rice is done, remove chicken and place it on a plate and set aside. Fluff rice with a serving spatula and maintain keep warm mode for 10 minutes. Remove bay leaves and discard. Remove the inner cooking pot from the rice cooker.
5. Portion rice into individual serving bowls or serving tray and place the chicken on top. Serve with blanched asparagus, peas, and pimiento.

CHICKEN JAMBALAYA WITH CHORIZO

This jambalaya and chorizo dish is my go-to recipe to serve up at a party or large family gathering. There isn't any occasion that won't be livened up with these rich, festive flavors, complete with garlic, pepper, and just enough Cajun seasonings to kick up the heat in every bite.

Recipe for 8 cup Rice Cooker and Food Steamer

Cooking time: 40 to 45 minutes

Yields: 4 to 6 cups

INGREDIENTS:

1 to 2 tablespoons of oil

2 chicken breasts fillets, excess fat trimmed and cubed

1 red onion, diced

1 red bell pepper, seeded and sliced into strips

2 garlic cloves, minced

¼ cup cooked chorizo, chopped

1 tablespoon of Cajun seasoning

2 cups of long-grain white rice

2 cups of canned stewed tomatoes, drained

Chicken stock, as needed to fill up to line 2

DIRECTIONS:

1. Rinse and drain the rice and place in a bowl, set aside. Season chicken with salt and pepper, place in a bowl and set aside.
2. Place the inner cooking pot in the rice cooker, turn on and press the white rice button to start cooking. Add and heat the oil in the inner cooking pot and brown the chicken on all sides while

stirring occasionally. Stir in the onions and cook for another 4 minutes or until the onions are soft and translucent. Add the minced garlic, tomatoes, chopped red pepper, chorizo and the Cajun seasoning. Cook for another 5 minutes, or until the ingredients are soft and the chorizo is cooked through. Remove from the inner cooking pot, place into a bowl and set aside.

3. Return the inner cooking pot in the rice cooker, add the drained rice and fill with chicken stock up to line 2. Close lid and wait until the rice is cooked through and switches to keep warm mode.

4. Once the rice is done, stir in half of chorizo mixture and half of the browned chicken. Fluff rice with a serving spatula and maintain in keep warm for 10 minutes.

5. Portion rice into individual serving bowls, serve warm with reserved chicken and chorizo mixture on top.

SPINACH, MUSHROOM, AND CHICKEN RISOTTO

If you're looking for a comfort-food dish that's as healthy as it is soothing, look no further than this delicious risotto. The vitamin-rich spinach and mushrooms are perfectly flavored with the chicken stock, and just a touch of Parmesan cheese ensures that the risotto will be creamy and savory down to the last bite. This is an ideal supper to serve at the end of a long day during the winter months, when everyone could use a little extra nutrients and warmth!

Recipe for 8-cup Rice Cooker and Food Steamer

Cooking time: 40 to 45 minutes

Yields: 4 to 6 cups

INGREDIENTS:

1 tablespoon extra-virgin olive oil

Salt and coarsely ground black pepper, to taste

2 chicken breast fillets, trimmed of fat and cut into 1-inch cubes

2 cups tightly packed spinach, washed and drained

Chicken stock, as needed to fill up to line 2

¼ cup Parmesan cheese, grated

2 cups of Arborio rice or any starchy short-grain rice variety, rinsed and drained

2 cups of Crimini or fresh shiitake mushrooms, sautéed ahead

DIRECTIONS:

1. Rinse and drain rice and place in a bowl, set aside. Season chicken with salt and pepper, set aside.
2. Place the inner cooking pot in the rice cooker, turn on and press the white rice button to start cooking. Add and heat the oil in the inner cooking pot, add the chicken and cook until lightly browned and cooked through. Remove from the inner cooking pot, place on a plate and set aside.
3. Return the inner cooking pot to the rice cooker, add the rice and fill with chicken stock up to line 2. Add the spinach on top, close the lid and wait until the rice is cooked through and switches to keep warm mode.
4. Once the rice is done, add in the mushrooms, ¾ of the chicken, and half of the grated cheese. Season to taste with salt and pepper, stir with serving spatula to combine and maintain keep warm mode for 10 minutes. Remove the inner cooking pot from the rice cooker.
5. Portion rice into individual serving bowls, serve warm with extra grated Parmesan and chicken pieces on top.

Greek Lemon Rice

This lightly seasoned, refreshing lemon-infused rice is an excellent base for any meal, particularly in the spring or summer months. That touch of sour citrus is perfectly tempered by the long-grain rice and stock, and the touch of rosemary in this preparation adds a depth of flavor to every bite.

Recipe for 8-cup Rice Cooker and Food Steamer

Cooking time: 40 to 45 minutes

Yields: 4 to 6 cups

INGREDIENTS:

2 cups of long-grain rice variety (Basmati or Jasmine rice), rinsed and drained

Chicken or vegetable stock, as needed to fill up to line 2

1 lemon, juiced

2 sprigs of fresh rosemary leaves

Salt and coarsely ground black pepper, to taste

Parsley leaves, chopped for garnish

DIRECTIONS:

1. Rinse and drain the rice, place in the inner cooking pot together with the stock, fresh lemon juice and sprigs of rosemary. Place the inner cooking pot in the rice cooker and close the lid, turn on and press the white rice button to start cooking.
2. Wait until the rice is cooked through and switches to keep warm mode. Fluff with a serving spatula, season to taste with salt and coarsely ground black pepper. Remove the rosemary and discard, close the lid and maintain keep warm mode for 10 minutes. Remove the inner cooking pot from the rice cooker.

MEDITERRANEAN BROWN RICE RECIPE

I got this recipe from a friend who lives in Sicily, though frankly I have no idea if the recipe is indigenous to the Italian island. All I know is that this flavorful, savory rice dish is a huge hit at my dinner parties and family gatherings – and that, to my great disappointment, I never seem to have any leftovers! Thank heavens it's incredibly easy to prepare.

Recipe for 8-cup Rice Cooker and Food Steamer

Cooking time: 75 to 80 minutes

Yields: 4 to 6 cups

INGREDIENTS:

2 cups brown rice, soaked and drained

Water or vegetable stock, as needed to fill up to line 2

1 medium bell pepper (red), seeded and sliced into strips

1 cup of canned green peas, drained

½ cup raisins

1 sweet onion, diced

¼ cup of green olives, sliced or halved

¼ cup of vegetable oil

¼ cup of balsamic vinegar

1 tablespoon of Dijon mustard

salt and coarsely ground black pepper, to taste

½ cup goat's or Feta cheese, crumbled

DIRECTIONS:

1. Drain the soaked rice and transfer into the inner cooking pot, fill with water or stock up to line 2. Place the inner cooking pot in the rice cooker, turn on and set the delay timer to the time when the rice is to be served. Press the brown rice button to cook.
4. While rice is cooking, in a mixing bowl, mix together the strips of bell pepper, the peas, onions, green olives and raisins. In a separate mixing bowl, whisk together the mustard, vinegar and oil until smooth and thick.
5. When the rice has completed the cooking process, add and mix the balsamic dressing and vegetable mixture in the pot with the cooked brown rice. Season with salt and black pepper and stir to combine. Allow to warm in keep warm mode for 10 minutes.
6. Portion into individual serving bowls or plates, serve warm with crumbled cheese on top.

WILD RICE WITH MUSHROOMS

This flavorful dish comes with all the tastes of early fall – and how sweet (or rather, savory!) it is. I love the combination of onion, mushrooms, and wild and long-grain rice, which is at once so elegant and yet so simple. The dash of wine and the chopped parsley in this dish add a real depth of flavor, and make this rice perfect to serve with the grilled meat or vegetable of your choice.

Recipe for 8-cup Rice Cooker and Food Steamer

Cooking time: 75 to 80 minutes

Yields: 4 to 6 cups

INGREDIENTS:

1 cup long-grain rice, rinsed and drained

1 cup wild rice, rinsed and drained

¼ cup of butter

Chicken or vegetable stock, as needed to fill up to line 2

1 large white onion, diced

1 cup of fresh mushrooms, trimmed and sliced or quartered

½ cup Marsala wine or dry sherry

1/2 cup loosely packed fresh flat-leaf parsley, coarsely chopped

Salt, to taste

DIRECTIONS:

1. Rinse and drain the long-grain and wild rice, place into a bowl and set aside.
2. Place the inner cooking pot in the rice cooker, turn on and press the brown rice button. Add and melt in the butter, sauté the onions until lightly brown and soft. Stir in the mushrooms and season with salt to taste, sauté until the mushrooms are cooked through and tender. Pour in the wine or dry sherry and cook until the liquid has been absorbed and evaporated. Remove from the inner pot, transfer to a bowl and set aside.
3. Place the mixed rice in the inner cooking pot and fill with stock up to line 2. Turn on rice cooker and press the brown rice button to start cooking. Cook and wait until the rice is done and cooked through, stir in the onion-mushroom mixture. Fluff with a serving spatula to combine and maintain keep warm mode for 10 minutes.
4. Portion into individual serving bowls or plates, serve warm with chopped parsley on top.

MEXICAN RICE

The lime juice, onion, cumin, and touch of cilantro are just enough to give this rice a perfect south-of-the-border tang. This is my favorite rice to serve up inside burritos, tacos, or any other Mexican-style feast. Of course, it also goes great with just about any meal – this rice really does pair up perfectly with all sorts of flavors, offering a neutral yet irresistible flavor base for all number of meats and veggies. It's wonderfully simple to prepare, and nutritious to boot thanks to the long-grain rice variety. So give it a try and serve it up – I know you'll be glad you did!

Recipe for 8-cup Rice Cooker and Food Steamer

Cooking time: 40 to 45 minutes

Yields: 4 to 6 cups

INGREDIENTS:

2 cups long-grain white rice, rinsed and drained

Chicken stock, as needed to fill up to line 2

1 tablespoon of oil

1 white onion, diced

3 garlic cloves, minced

3 to 4 tablespoons of tomato paste

1 organic lime, juiced

½ cup loosely packed fresh cilantro, coarsely chopped

½ tablespoon of cumin powder

Salt, to taste

DIRECTIONS:

1. Rinse and drain the rice, place in a bowl and set aside.
2. Place the inner cooking pot in the rice cooker, turn on and press the white rice button to start cooking. Add and heat the oil, add the diced onions and sauté until lightly brown and translucent. Stir in the minced garlic and cook until fragrant while stirring occasionally. Stir in the cumin powder and tomato paste and cook for 2 minutes more, stirring regularly. Remove from the inner cooking pot, place into a bowl and set aside.
3. Return the inner cooking pot to the rice cooker, add rice and fill with chicken stock up to line 2. Turn on and press the white rice button to start cooking. Close lid and wait until the rice is cooked and ready. Once the rice is done, stir in the tomato paste mixture, lime juice and ¾ of the chopped cilantro and then fluff with a serving spatula to combine. Season to taste with salt and maintain in keep warm mode for 10 minutes. Remove the inner cooking pot from the rice cooker.
4. Portion into individual serving bowls, serve warm with chopped cilantro on top.

DOMINICAN-STYLE YELLOW RICE

The blend of spices and seasonings in this rice are what make it truly special. I love the way the garlic, scallions, cumin, turmeric and pepper all work together to create a wonderfully layered savory flavor blend, and the colorful presentation of this dish makes it especially fun to serve at any meal. This dish goes great with the meat or veggie dish of your choice, so don't be shy and give it a try!

Recipe for 8-cup Rice Cooker and Food Steamer

Cooking time: 40 to 45 minutes

Yields: 4 to 6 cups

INGREDIENTS:

1 tablespoon of oil

1 red onion, diced

1 green bell pepper, seeded and sliced into strips

2 celery ribs, roughly chopped

2 medium scallions, bias cuts

2 to 3 garlic cloves, minced

1 bay leaf

½ tablespoon of cumin seeds

½ tablespoon of ground turmeric

½ teaspoon of cayenne pepper

2 cups of long-grain rice, rinsed and drained

Chicken stock, as needed to fill up to line 2

Salt, to taste

¼ cup loosely packed fresh cilantro, chopped

½ cup loosely packed fresh flat leaf parsley, chopped

DIRECTIONS:

1. Rinse and drain the rice, place in a bowl and set aside.
2. Place the inner cooking pot in the rice cooker, turn on and press the white rice button to start cooking. Add the oil, diced onions, green pepper, scallions and chopped celery and cook until soft, while stirring occasionally. Stir in the minced garlic, cumin, turmeric powder, cayenne pepper and the bay leaf and cook until the ingredients are evenly mixed.
3. Stir in the drained rice, fill with chicken stock up to line 2 and then season with salt. Briefly stir to combine the ingredients and close lid. Cook and wait until the rice is cooked through. Once the rice is done, fluff with a serving spatula and maintain in keep warm mode for 10 minutes. Remove inner cooking pot from the rice cooker.
4. Portion rice into individual serving bowls, serve warm with chopped cilantro and parsley on top.

SULLIVAN'S ISLAND BACON AND SHRIMP BOG

Talk about surf-and-turf – with a twist! This dish, native to a small island in South Carolina, is truly sensational. With bacon, shrimp, long-grain rice and a tangy-savory blend of spices and seasonings, this dish is a serious feast. I love serving this dish at parties or family gatherings – there's just something deeply festive about these rich flavors and succulent meats. If you've got a party coming up – or just a meal that you want to feel extra-special – I urge you to give this delicious recipe a try.

Recipe for 8-cup Rice Cooker and Food Steamer

Cooking time: 40 to 45 minutes

Yields: 4 to 6 cups

INGREDIENTS:

1 cup diced smoked bacon

2 red onions, diced

2 cups of long-grain rice, rinsed and drained

Chicken stock, as needed to fill up to line 2

2 ripe red tomatoes, diced

1 organic lemon, juiced

1 to 2 tablespoons of Worcestershire sauce

½ teaspoon salt, to taste

A pinch of black pepper, coarsely ground

A pinch of cayenne pepper

A pinch of ground nutmeg

2 to 3 cups of fresh shrimp, peeled and deveined

¼ cup loosely packed fresh parsley leaves, minced

DIRECTIONS:

1. Rinse and drain the rice, place in a bowl and set aside.
2. Place the inner pot in the rice cooker, turn on and press the white rice button to start cooking. Add the bacon and cook until crispy. Remove from inner pot and transfer to a plate lined with paper towels to drain excess oil, leaving the cooking fat in the pot. When the bacon has cooled, chop it into small pieces.
3. Add the onions to the pot and cook until soft and translucent, add the drained rice and stir thoroughly to coat evenly with oil. Fill the inner pot with stock up to line 2 and stir in the diced tomatoes, juice of lemon, cayenne, ground nutmeg, Worcestershire sauce and season to taste with salt and pepper. Return ¾ of bacon to the inner cooking pot and add the shrimp. Briefly stir the ingredients to combine and close the lid. Wait until the rice is cooked through.
4. Once the rice is done, fluff with a serving spatula and maintain in keep warm mode for 10 minutes.
5. Portion into individual serving bowls, serve warm with chopped parsley, shrimp and bacon on top.

Dirty Rice

Don't let the name fool you – this "dirty" rice (so called because of its colorfully hodgepodge appearance) is filled with good clean nutrients, vegetables, scrumptious savory pork sausage and just the right mix of seasonings to really give each bite a kick. This traditional Cajun rice dish has gained popularity around the world, and you'll understand exactly why with the first bite.

Recipe for 8-cup Rice Cooker and Food Steamer

Cooking time: 40 to 45 minutes

Yields: 4 to 6 cups

INGREDIENTS:

4 links of spicy pork sausage, casings removed and chopped

1 red onion, diced

2 medium celery stalks, chopped

4 garlic cloves, minced

1 medium green bell pepper, seeded and diced

2 cups long-grain white rice, rinsed and drained

¼ teaspoon black pepper, coarsely ground to taste

1 tablespoon of Tabasco sauce or hot chili sauce

½ tablespoon of Cajun Seasoning, as needed for extra heat

Salt, to taste

Beef stock, as need to fill up to line 2

2 green onions, roughly chopped

DIRECTIONS:

1. Rinse and drain the rice, place in a bowl and set aside.
2. Place the inner cooking pot in the rice cooker, turn on and press the white rice button to start cooking. Add the sausage and cook until it starts to brown, stir in the garlic, diced onions, chopped celery and bell pepper and cook until the vegetables are tender and the sausage is cooked through.
3. Add the Cajun seasoning, Tabasco or hot chili sauce and coarsely ground black pepper and stir well to combine. Remove from the inner pot, transfer to a large bowl and set aside.
4. Place the rice in the inner cooking pot and fill with beef stock up to line 2. Return the cooked ingredients, stir to combine and close the lid, wait until the rice is fully cooked.
5. Once the rice is done, fluff with a serving spatula and maintain in keep warm mode for 10 minutes. Season to taste with extra salt and Tabasco sauce, if desired.
6. Portion into individual serving bowls, serve warm with chopped green onions and extra sausage on top.

6

BREAKFAST RECIPES

Giant Pancake

Show me a person who doesn't love pancakes for breakfast, and I'll show you an extraterrestrial alien in disguise. In other words, everyone loves pancakes for breakfast – and there's no more fun or scrumptious way to prepare them than in the rice-cooker, which allows you to make a huge giant pancake without the mess and fuss of unwieldy stovetop pans. These giant pancakes come out light, fluffy, moist and perfect every time – and they're as much fun to eat as they are to prepare, so have at it and get ready to give your family a real breakfast treat!

Preparation time: 5 minutes

Cooking time: 45 minutes

Yields: 4

INGREDIENTS:

1 cup of flour, sifted

2 tablespoons white sugar

1 teaspoon baking powder

½ teaspoon baking soda

½ teaspoon salt

1 large whole egg

¾ cup fresh milk

2 tablespoons butter, unsalted and melted

Maple syrup, for serving (optional)

Fresh fruit, for serving (optional)

DIRECTIONS:

1. Mix together the sifted flour, salt, sugar, baking powder and baking soda in a mixing bowl. Set aside.
2. In a separate mixing bowl, whisk together the milk, egg and melted butter until smooth. Add the wet mixture into the bowl with the dry mixture, mix to combine.
3. Lightly brush the inner cooking pot with oil or butter and place into the rice cooker, turn on and press the white rice button to start cooking. When the oil is hot, pour the mixture into the inner cooking pot. Close lid and cook for 45 minutes, or until browned and cooked through.
4. When the pancake is done, switch to keep warm mode and test doneness. When a toothpick inserted in the thickest part comes out clean, it is done.
5. Remove the inner cooking pot from the rice cooker and turn over to flip pancake onto a serving plate. Let it rest for 5 minutes before serving.
6. Slice the pancake and serve with maple syrup and fresh fruit on top, if desired.

Scrambled Eggs with Tomatoes

This balanced and savory breakfast is the perfect dish to serve up on a weekday morning, filled with protein to supercharge the day and give your family the energy they need. I love that this recipe incorporates both bacon and ham, and of course the eggs and onions come out cooked to perfection in the rice-cooker, in a way that I never seem to manage on the stovetop. This breakfast is one of my favorite go-to weekday morning dishes, and I trust you'll love it as much as I do.

Preparation time: 5 minutes

Cooking time: 15 to 20 minutes

Yields: 2

INGREDIENTS:

2 medium whole eggs

1 tablespoon clarified butter

2 ripe red tomatoes, peeled and diced

2 tablespoons of crispy bacon bits

2 tablespoons diced ham

Salt and pepper, to taste

1 tablespoon green onion (optional)

2 tablespoons of grated Parmesan cheese (for serving)

DIRECTIONS:

1. Place the inner cooking pot into the rice cooker, turn on and press the white rice button to start cooking. Add the clarified butter and stir in the bacon bits and diced ham. Cook for 1 to 2 minutes while stirring regularly. Stir in the diced tomatoes and cook for 5 more minutes while stirring occasionally.

2. While cooking the meats and tomatoes, lightly beat the eggs in a bowl and add into the inner pot.
3. Briefly stir the eggs and meats, season to taste with salt and pepper and close the lid securely. Cook for 10 to 15 minutes or until the bottom part is lightly browned and the eggs are cooked through. Switch to keep warm mode and flip to cook the other side, if needed.
4. Remove eggs from the inner cooking pot, transfer to a serving dish and serve warm with grated cheese and green onion on top.

RICE PUDDING

There is, to my thinking, no dessert more simple, sweet and comforting than a bowl of classic rice pudding. Little surprise, of course, that my favorite method of preparing it would be in my trusty rice-cooker. This recipe keeps things classic and traditional, with just a pinch of cinnamon to bring out that old-timey flavor. This recipe is a must-have for any cook's dessert files, so keep it close – if your family's dessert tastes are anything like mine, you'll be getting frequent requests for this sweet treat!

Preparation time: 10 minutes

Cooking time: 20 minutes

Yields: 4

INGREDIENTS:

2 1/2 cups skim milk

1 cups short-grain white rice, rinsed and drained

½ cup white sugar

A pinch of cinnamon powder

1 cup of skim milk, for serving

DIRECTIONS:

1. Rinse and drain the rice, place into the inner cooking pot together with 2 1/2 cups of milk, sugar and cinnamon. Place the inner cooking pot into the rice cooker, turn on and press the white rice button to start cooking. Close the lid securely and cook until the rice cooker switches to keep warm mode, or about 20 minutes.
2. Stir in 1 cup of milk and let it rest for 5 minutes before serving. Portion into individual serving bowls and serve warm with chocolate sauce on top, if preferred.

Rice Cooker Ham and Eggs

Ham and eggs is a surefire breakfast winner, a classic the world over for very good reason. But if you've never tried to cook it in your rice cooker, I strongly recommend this method – so much simpler, cleaner, and faster than messing around with pots and pans on the stovetop, and every bit as delectably irresistible as the traditional dish we all know and love. Green eggs and ham may have their mystique, but rice-cooker-cooked eggs and ham are the winner by far.

Preparation time: 5 minutes

Cooking time: 10 to 15 minutes

Yields: 4 to 6

INGREDIENTS:

8 medium whole eggs

½ cup heavy whipping cream

½ cup cooked ham, diced

1 green onion, roughly chopped

A pinch salt, to taste

A pinch of ground black pepper

1 to 2 tablespoons of melted butter

¼ cup of cream cheese

DIRECTIONS:

1. Whisk together the eggs and cream in a mixing bowl, stir in the ham and onions. Season to taste with salt and pepper and set aside.
2. Place the inner cooking pot in the rice cooker, turn on and press the white rice button to start cooking. Melt the butter in the pot and pour in the egg-cream mixture. Briefly stir the ingredients and cook until the mixture is set, or for about 10 to 15 minutes.
3. When the egg and cream mixture is ready, stir in the cream cheese and maintain keep warm mode for 5 minutes.
4. Remove from the inner pot and transfer to a serving plate or portion into individual serving plates. Serve warm with extra cheese and onions on top if desired.

BREAKFAST OATMEAL

We all know that classic breakfast oatmeal is an excellent and nutritious way to start the day off right. But did you know how fast and foolproof it is to prepare in your very own rice-cooker? This recipe is my go-to favorite for this breakfast staple, and my family absolutely loves it. So forget about instant-mix oatmeals or fancy stovetop gimmicks; with this tried and true recipe and a good rice-cooker, you're good to go for hot oatmeal and a great morning!

Preparation time: 5 minutes

Cooking time: 25 minutes

Yields: 3 to 4

INGREDIENTS:

1 cup rolled oats

1 ½ cups of milk, or as needed

½ teaspoon almond extract

1 teaspoon cinnamon

1 pinch salt

¼ cup maple syrup, divided

½ cup dates, chopped for serving

DIRECTIONS:

1. Add and mix all ingredients into the inner cooking pot, place the inner cooking pot into the rice cooker. Turn on and press the white rice button to start cooking.
2. Cook until the rice cooker switches to keep warm mode, or until the oats have absorbed most of the liquid. Adjust consistency by

adding more milk if the porridge is too thick. Maintain in keep warm mode for 5 minutes before serving.

3. Remove from the inner cooking pot and portion into individual serving bowls. Serve warm with extra maple syrup and chopped dates on top.

KOREAN-STYLE SCALLION PANCAKES

If you've never tried Korean-style savory pancakes, this scallion-centric recipe is a great place to start. Tangy and slightly spicy in that delicate way that scallions have, these pancakes are a scrumptious way to start the day, or an elegant addition to brunch or even dinner. All my friends, family, and guests love these sophisticated savory pancakes, and I know yours will too.

Preparation time: 10 minutes

Cooking time: 10 to 15 minutes

Yields: 2 to 4

INGREDIENTS:

10 stems of scallions, cut into long pieces

½ cup flour, sifted

½ cup water

½ teaspoon soybean paste

½ teaspoon sugar

2 to 3 tablespoons vegetable oil

DIRECTIONS:

1. Mix the flour and sugar in bowl, and mix in the water and soybean paste. Mix the ingredients thoroughly until well combined.
2. Place the inner cooking pot in the rice cooker, turn on and press the white rice button to start cooking. Add the oil. Place and arrange the scallions in the pot to form a square or rectangle. Pour the batter on the bed of green onions. Cook the pancake until the bottom is browned and crispy while slightly pressing down with a spatula.

3. Turn to cook the other side and close the lid. Switch to keep warm mode, wait for 10 minutes and open lid. Remove from the inner cooking pot and transfer it to a serving plate. Let it rest for 5 minutes to cool, and slice the pancake into 2 or 4 equal portions.
4. Serve warm with preferred sauce.

Asian Beef Crepes

These savory beef crepes are a wonderful twist on the old brunch classic, filled with delicious savory beef and seasoned vegetables. Adding the chili paste or crushed red pepper brings the perfect amount of spice to this dish, and the ginger and fish sauce in the meat marinade work together perfectly for a flavor combination that's layered, complex, and simply delicious!

Preparation time: 15 minutes

Cooking time: 20 to 25 minutes

Yields: 10

INGREDIENTS:

2 ounces uncooked rice sticks (rice flour noodles)

1 teaspoon vegetable oil

1 tablespoon fresh lime juice

1/2 teaspoon chili paste or crushed red pepper

10 medium Boston lettuce leaves

10 Basic Crepes

1/2 cup shredded carrot

30 thinly cut slices seeded cucumber

30 mint leaves

30 cilantro sprigs

Marinade

1 1/2 tablespoons fish sauce

1 tablespoon minced peeled fresh ginger

2 teaspoons sugar

1 flank steak, sliced into thin strips

DIRECTIONS:

1. Combine together all ingredients for the marinade, transfer to a resealable plastic bag and add the steak. Chill for at least 2 hours to allow the marinade mixture to penetrate into the meat.
2. Place the rice sticks in a large bowl and cover with boiling water. Set aside and drain before use.
3. Place the inner cooking pot in the rice cooker, turn on and press the white rice button to start cooking. Add the beef and cook for 4 minutes while stirring regularly. Pour in the marinade and add the soaked rice sticks, lime juice and chili paste. Close the lid and cook for 10 minutes, switch to keep warm mode and set aside for 15 minutes to cook with low heat. Remove from heat and set aside.
4. Place the crepes on a work surface and place a lettuce leaf on each. Top with beef and chopped vegetables and roll it up. Repeat procedure with the remaining crepes.
5. Cut each roll into 3 equal portions, and serve with your favorite dipping sauce.

THAI MANGO WITH COCONUT STICKY RICE

If you're hankering for a sweet daytime treat, this mango-infused, coconut-laden sticky rice simply can't be beat. This is a wonderful and deceptively simple aromatic preparation that lets each individual flavor shine, and makes a filling and crowd-pleasing meal for breakfast, brunch, or anytime you want a dish that's as sweet as it is wholesome.

Preparation time: 10 minutes

Cooking time: 55 to 60 minutes

Yields: 4

INGREDIENTS:

2 cups sticky rice, soaked and drained

1 ½ cups canned coconut milk

¼ cup white sugar, divided

½ teaspoon salt

½ cup coconut cream, for serving

2 ripe mangoes, pitted and sliced into short and thin slices

Toasted sesame seeds, for serving

Fresh mint leaves, for serving

DIRECTIONS:

1. In a mixing bowl, place the rice and add water to cover. Soak for an hour, rinse with running water and drain.
2. Slowly transfer the coconut milk to a glass bowl and let it stand for 5 minutes. When the thicker liquid or the cream has risen above the mixture, scoop it out and place it in a separate bowl. Set aside.

3. Place the soaked sticky rice into the inner cooking pot, add ½ cup of water, half the sugar and the thinner coconut mixture left in the glass bowl. Briefly stir the ingredients and place the inner cooking pot in the rice cooker, turn on and press the white rice button to start cooking. Close the lid and cook for 20 minutes, or until most of the liquid has been absorbed by the rice.

4. When the rice has absorbed most of the liquid, pour the reserved coconut cream into the inner cooking pot. Add the salt and stir the ingredients until well incorporated. Cook for another 10 minutes or until the liquid has been fully absorbed. Switch to keep warm mode and cook for another 10 minutes. Remove from the inner cooking pot and transfer to a bowl, cover and set aside.

5. While the rice is in the final cooking stage, prepare the coconut sauce for serving. Wash the inner cooking pot and wipe it with cloth, return into the rice cooker and press the white rice button to cook. Pour ½ cup coconut cream in the inner cooking pot and add the remaining sugar. Cook for 5 minutes while stirring regularly, or until the sugar has been completely dissolved. Remove the inner cooking pot, transfer to a bowl and set aside.

6. Portion the coconut sticky rice into individual serving plates or bowls. Top with mango slices and pour the creamy coconut sauce on each serving. Serve warm with toasted sesame seeds and fresh mint leaves on top.

Brown Rice Congee with Shiitake Mushrooms

Shitake mushrooms are not only an excellent source of b-vitamins and other essential minerals and nutrients. They're also a purely delectable feature for a breakfast or brunch meal, provided of course, that they're given the right seasoning treatment. This recipe uses ginger, garlic, bok choy, scallions, peanuts, and a touch of soy sauce and chili to perfectly showcase these most delicious of fungi. This is a scrumptious and hearty vegetarian meal that's perfect for any morning of the week, so serve it up and get your fill!

Preparation time: 10 minutes

Cooking time: 2 hours 20 minutes

Yields: 2 to 4

INGREDIENTS:

1 tablespoon cooking oil

2 garlic cloves, crushed and thinly sliced

1-inch fresh ginger root, peeled and julienned

1 cup fresh shiitake mushrooms, halved

1 cups long-grain brown rice, soaked, rinsed and drained

4 cups chicken or vegetable stock

1 head of Bok Choy, chopped

Soy sauce and chili paste, to taste

Ground black pepper, to taste

Scallions, chopped for serving

Roasted peanuts, for serving

DIRECTIONS:

1. Rinse and drain the soaked brown rice, place in a bowl and set aside.
2. Place the inner cooking pot in the rice cooker, turn on and press the white rice button to start cooking. Add and heat the oil, sauté the garlic and ginger for 5 minutes or until browned and fragrant while stirring occasionally. Stir in the mushrooms and cook for 2 minutes, or until soft.
3. Add the rice and stock in the inner cooking pot. Place the inner pot in the rice cooker and turn it on. Set the delay timer with 2 hours or more to soak and soften the brown rice, and then press the brown rice button to start cooking. Close lid securely and wait until the rice cooker switches to keep warm mode.
4. Check consistency of rice congee and season to taste with soy sauce, black pepper and chili paste, as desired. If you want to have a thicker soup consistency, press the brown rice button and cook for another 10 minutes or until the desired consistency is achieved. Switch to keep warm mode and let it stand for 5 minutes. Remove the inner cooking pot from the rice cooker.
5. Portion the rice congee into individual serving bowls. Serve warm with chopped scallions and roasted peanuts on top.

SOUTHEAST ASIAN CREPES WITH CUMIN SEEDS

These wonderful curry-flavored crepes are exotic brunch at its finest. The coriander and cumin create an outstanding flavor blend with the crepe dough, for a taste that is both complex and rich, yet elegant and delicate. This is a wonderful breakfast or brunch to serve when you're looking to impress – trust me, these crepes won't let you down.

Preparation time: 10 minutes

Cooking time: 15 minutes

Yields: 4

INGREDIENTS:

1 cup all-purpose flour

¼ cup rice flour

¼ cup loosely packed curry leaves, chopped

¼ cup loosely packed fresh coriander leaves, chopped

½ tablespoon of cumin seeds, crushed

1 teaspoon salt

2 cups of water

2 tablespoons of butter

Whip cream, for serving

Fresh fruits, sliced

DIRECTIONS:

1. Combine together the rice flour, all-purpose flour, cumin seeds and salt in a mixing bowl. Mix in the chopped curry and coriander leaves and pour in the water. Continue mixing until well incorporated.

2. Place the inner cooking pot in the rice cooker, turn on and press the white rice button to start cooking.

3. Add and melt 1 tablespoon of butter in the inner cooking pot. Once the butter has melted, slowly pour the batter mixture in the inner pot. Add just enough batter just to cover the bottom of the pan. Cook the crepe until the bottom is lightly browned and turn to cook the other side for 2 minutes. Repeat the procedure with the remaining batter and the remaining butter if needed.

4. Place the crepes on individual serving plates. Serve with whip cream and fresh fruit slices on top.

SHAKSHUKA

This rich, savory poached egg dish is traditional in much of the Middle East, and I daresay it goes down as a serious treat for breakfast or brunch anywhere else on the planet as well. The egg and zucchini are perfectly flavored with this awesome blend of spices and seasonings cooked in a tomato base, and the best part is that this is a wonderfully healthy way to start the day. Filled with lean protein and nutrient-rich legumes, this dish is a total winner. Now, what's Arabic for "More, please?"

Preparation time: 10 minutes

Cooking time: 25 minutes

Yields: 2

INGREDIENTS:

½ tablespoon oil

2 garlic cloves, minced

1 medium onion, diced

1 medium zucchini, peeled and diced

1 cup canned crushed tomatoes

hot pepper sauce, as needed for added heat

4 medium eggs

a pinch of salt and ground black pepper, to taste

Fresh parsley, chopped for garnish

DIRECTIONS:

1. Place the inner cooking pot in the rice cooker, turn on and press the white rice button to start cooking. Add and heat the oil in the inner cooking pot. Add the onion and garlic, sauté until soft and fragrant. Stir in the zucchini, tomato sauce and the hot pepper sauce in the inner pot. Cook for 3 minutes or until the vegetables are tender and the liquid has reduced, stirring occasionally.
2. Season to taste with salt and black pepper. Provide 4 spaces or make wells in the vegetable mixture, crack the eggs and carefully place one at a time in each well. Close lid and switch to keep warm mode, cook until the whites are set and the yellows are still runny. Do not stir the mixture.
3. When the eggs are ready and set, remove the inner cooking pot from the rice cooker. Let it stand for 5 minutes.
4. Transfer the Shaksuka on a serving plate, serve warm with chopped parsley on top.

POTATOES WITH EGGS AND SPICED TOMATO SAUCE

This is a hearty Moroccan-spiced rendition of the classic breakfast fry-up, loaded with sausage, onion, potatoes, eggs, and just enough cilantro and garlic to ensure that every bite is tangy with a touch of the exotic. This is a great weekend breakfast or brunch to serve when you've got the whole family gathered around your table – it's perfect for sharing, and will put everyone in the mood for family fun.

Preparation time: 15 minutes

Cooking time: 45 minutes

Yields: 4

INGREDIENTS:

2 tablespoons oil

1 medium onion, diced

5 garlic cloves, minced

3 links of hot Italian sausage, casings removed and chopped

½ pound potatoes, peeled, halved lengthwise and thinly sliced

1 tablespoon Moroccan spice mixture (Ras el hanout)

Salt, to taste

2 cups canned crushed tomatoes

1 tablespoon hot chili pepper paste

4 eggs

Fresh Cilantro leaves, chopped for garnish (optional)

DIRECTIONS:

1. Place the inner cooking pot in the rice cooker, turn on and press the white rice button to start cooking. Add and heat the oil in the inner cooking pot, add the onions and sauté until tender and translucent. Stir in the garlic and sauté for 2 minutes until brown and fragrant.
2. Stir in the sausage and cook for 5 minutes, or until browned and cooked through. Mix in the potatoes and season to taste with salt and Ras el hanout. Briefly stir the ingredient, close the lid and cook until the potatoes are soft and cooked through. Flip the potatoes occasionally to ensure even cooking. Stir in the crushed tomatoes and chili paste, cook for 5 minutes while stirring occasionally.
3. Provide four spaces or make wells in the tomato-potato mixture, crack the eggs and carefully place an egg in each well. Close the lid and switch to keep warm mode, let it cook for about 5 minutes, or until the whites are set and the yellows are still runny. Remove the inner cooking pot from the rice cooker.
4. Transfer the potato and tomato mixture to a serving plate. Serve with chopped cilantro on top.

LEBANESE PITAS WITH MEAT STUFFING

These meat-filled pitas are a fantastic savory feast that the whole family will love. The meat is perfectly seasoned with parsley, onion, garlic, tomato, a touch of masala and pine nuts, and lemon juice to help keep every bite succulent and tender. This dish is always a huge hit with my friends and family, and I know you'll get a great reaction too. The best part is how simple and fast it is to whip up in the rice-cooker, so have at it!

Preparation time: 25 minutes

Cooking time: 20 minutes

Yields: 4

INGREDIENTS:

1 small white onion, finely minced

1 garlic clove, finely minced

¼ cup loosely packed fresh parsley, finely minced

½ pound lean beef, ground

1 ripe tomato, diced

A pinch of garam masala

¼ cup pine nuts, toasted

½ lemon, juiced

Salt, to taste

2 pita rounds, cut into quarters

1 ½ tablespoon olive oil, for greasing

DIRECTIONS:

2. Place the inner cooking pot in the rice cooker, turn on and press the white rice button to start cooking. Add and heat 1 tablespoon of oil in the pot, add and sauté the garlic and onion until soft and fragrant. Stir in the beef, garam masala and salt to taste. Cook for 5 to 7 minutes, or until the beef is browned and cooked through while stirring occasionally. Remove from the inner pot and place in a bowl, set aside to cool.

5. Mix in the parsley, tomato, lemon juice and pine nuts with the beef mixture. Stir to combine.

6. Place 4 pita quarters on a work surface, add 2 tablespoons of beef mixture on each slice and cover with another slice of pita.

7. Wipe the inner pot with cloth or paper towel and return into the rice cooker. Press the white rice button and heat in the remaining oil. Place the stuffed pita quarters in the pot, cover and cook for about 5 to 7 minutes, or until the bottom part is browned. Carefully flip the stuffed pitas and switch to keep warm mode. Maintain in keep warm mode before serving.

8. Remove the stuffed warm pitas from the inner cooking pot and transfer to a serving plate. Serve warm with Greek yogurt if desired.

SPINACH AND FETA GOZLEME

This traditional Turkish flatbread dish is an absolute dream, and the perfect savory treat to start off the day or to mark a celebratory brunch. I love the combination of goat's cheese and mozzarella, which create the perfect flavor infusion for the spinach inside that delicate flatbread dough. Serve this dish anytime you want to impress your breakfast or brunch guests with a meal that's both sophisticated and scrumptious.

Preparation time: 30 minutes

Cooking time: 10 minutes

Yields: 4

INGREDIENTS:

For the spinach

1 cup tightly packed fresh spinach

½ onion, diced

2 tablespoons olive oil

Salt and ground black pepper, to taste

¼ cup goat's cheese, crumbled

¼ cup Mozzarella cheese, shredded

For the dough

2 cups flour, sifted

1 cup of water

½ teaspoon salt

DIRECTIONS:

1. Combine the flour and salt in a mixing bowl, gradually pour in the water while mixing until the mixture comes together and doesn't stick to the side of the bowl. Transfer into a floured work surface and knead for about 5 minutes or until smooth and elastic. Roll out the dough and form into a ball, return into the bowl and cover with cloth. Let it rest for about 10 to 15 minutes.
2. While the dough is resting, place the inner cooking pot in the rice cooker, turn on and press the white rice button to start cooking. Add and heat 1 tablespoon of oil in the inner pot, add the onions and sauté until soft and fragrant. Stir in the spinach, season to taste with salt and ground pepper and cook until the spinach leaves are wilted. Close lid and switch to keep warm mode.
3. Bring the dough to the floured work surface and divide it into 4 equal portions. Roll out each portion into thin rounds.
4. Portion the spinach mixture into 4 and add it on the center of the dough. Top with goat's and Mozzarella cheese and fold the dough into half, bringing the opposite sides. Repeat the procedure with the remaining ingredients.
5. Wipe the inner cooking pot with paper towels and return it into the rice cooker. Press the white rice button and add the remaining oil. Place the first 2 stuffed dough pockets in the inner pot and cook for about 7 minutes, or until browned. Flip it over to cook the other side for another 5 minutes. Remove from the inner cooking pot and cook the remaining stuffed dough. Return the gozlemes that have been cooked earlier to the inner pot and switch to keep warm mode. Maintain keep warm mode before serving.
6. Remove the gozlemes from the inner cooking pot, cut each into 2 portions. Transfer to a serving platter and serve with preferred dipping sauce.

MUSHROOM FRITTATA

I love a good frittata, and this mushroom frittata is as scrumptious as they come. It's also a terrific source of b-vitamins, with which mushrooms are loaded, and the onions, rosemary and nutmeg in this recipe create the perfect flavor balance to make every bite as delicious as it is nutritious. This is an elegant dish that will help elevate any breakfast or brunch, perfect for family gatherings or daytime parties.

Preparation time: 10 minutes

Cooking time: 35 minutes

Yields: 6

INGREDIENTS:

5 whole eggs

2 egg whites

¼ cup loosely packed fresh parsley, roughly chopped

½ teaspoon salt, divided

½ teaspoon black pepper, coarsely ground, divided

A pinch of nutmeg

½ tablespoon olive oil

3 red onions, diced

1 teaspoon of dried rosemary

2 cups mixed mushrooms, quartered

½ cup Parmesan cheese, grated

4 thin slices of Italian ham, diced

DIRECTIONS:

1. Place the inner cooking pot in the rice cooker, turn on and press the white rice button to start cooking. Add and heat the oil in the inner cooking pot, add the onions and sauté until soft and translucent. Season to taste with salt and pepper, and then stir in the rosemary and mushrooms. Close the lid and cook for another 8 to 10 minutes, or until the mushrooms are soft and cooked through.
2. While cooking the vegetables, whisk together the eggs and egg whites until well combined. Whisk in the parsley, nutmeg and season to taste with salt and pepper.
3. Pour the egg mixture over the vegetable mixture, cook for about 4 minutes and top with grated Parmesan cheese and diced ham. Close lid and switch to keep warm mode to continue cooking with low heat and to melt the cheese. Remove the frittata from the inner cooking pot just before serving.
4. To serve the mushroom frittata, remove it from the inner pot and cut into 6 equal slices. Transfer to a serving plate and serve with your favorite sauce.

LITHUANIAN PANCAKE RECIPE

These traditional Lithuanian pancakes take the standard western preparation and add the delicious twist of whipped cream, fresh fruit and honey. This is a fantastic breakfast to prepare on weekends or special occasions – a birthday, perhaps – that is as good to look at as it is to eat. My whole family cheers when I whip up a batch of these, and I know yours will love them just as much.

Preparation time: 10 minutes

Cooking time: 55 to 60 minutes

Yields: 4 to 6

INGREDIENTS:

1 package of basic pancake mix (including ingredients to prepare mixture according to the box)

Whipped cream, for serving

½ tablespoon cooking oil, for greasing

Fresh strawberries and kiwi, sliced for serving

Honey, for serving

DIRECTIONS:

1. Prepare the pancake mixture according to package directions, set aside.
2. Place the inner cooking pot in the rice cooker, turn on and press the white rice button to start cooking. Wait until the inner cooking pot is very hot, and then add the oil.
3. Pour the batter mixture in the inner cooking pot. Close lid and cook for about 40 to 50 minutes, or until the top part is no longer wet. It is done when a toothpick inserted on the thickest part

comes out clean. Switch to keep warm mode, and let it cook for 10 minutes more with low heat.

4. Remove the inner cooking pot from the rice cooker. Place a plate on top and turn it over to remove the pancake. Let it rest for 5 to 10 minutes before serving.
5. Slice the pancake and top with fresh fruit slices. Drizzle with honey on top and serve warm.

TORTILLA ESPANOLA

This traditional Spanish egg-and-potato dish is an ideal breakfast or brunch, though it will also work great as a side-dish for an evening meal. This recipe keeps the flavors wonderfully simple, with just a touch of onion, salt and pepper to kick up the taste, meaning this dish will taste great on its own or with the meat and vegetable dishes of your choice.

Preparation time: 10 minutes

Cooking time: 35 minutes

Yields: 6 to 8

INGREDIENTS:

½ cup oil, or as needed

4 medium potatoes, peeled and thinly sliced

1 white onion, minced

Salt and ground pepper, to taste

5 whole eggs

DIRECTIONS:

1. Place the inner cooking pot in the rice cooker, turn on and press the white rice button to start cooking. Wait until the inner cooking pot is very hot and then add 1 tbsp oil. Place the onions in the inner pot and sauté until soft and translucent. Stir in the potatoes and several tablespoons of oil so all potatoes have a light coat of oil. Cook for about 10 minutes while stirring occasionally. Add more oil if necessary. When the potatoes are tender and cooked through, season to taste with salt and pepper.
2. Add the eggs in a mixing bowl and whisk briefly. Pour the egg mixture in the inner pot with the potatoes, and cook for 10 minutes. With a tong and spatula, carefully flip it over to cook the

other side. Close the lid, switch to keep warm mode and cook for about 10 to 15 minutes.

3. Remove the inner cooking pot from the rice cooker and let it rest for 5 minutes before serving.
4. Slice into 6 or 8 equal portions, serve warm.

Chorizo Hash Browns

These chorizo hash browns are a seriously indulgent dish to serve at breakfast or brunch on special occasions. The way the natural oils from the bacon and chorizo help to perfectly season the potatoes and tomatoes is pure perfection, and I particularly love the way these hash browns come out crispy and delicious in my rice cooker. I won't pretend that this is the healthiest breakfast dish on the block, but it sure is a contender for the most delicious – so go on and give these pork-laden hash browns a try, because they really are worth it.

Preparation time: 5 minutes

Cooking time: 15 minutes

Yields: 2 to 4

INGREDIENTS:

6 baby potatoes, skin on

3 strips of bacon, diced

1 link chorizo, sliced into thin rounds

1 cup of cherry tomatoes, halved

2 whole eggs

2 to 3 tablespoons of water

1 teaspoon oil

Salt and ground black pepper, to taste

1 avocado, pitted and sliced (optional)

Fresh parsley leaves, minced for garnish

Crusty bread, for serving

DIRECTIONS:

1. Place the inner cooking pot in the rice cooker and add the potatoes. Add water in the inner pot to cover the potatoes, turn on the rice cooker and press the white rice button to start cooking. Boil the potatoes until soft, remove from the inner cooking pot. Rinse with cool running water to cool down. Cut the potatoes into half and set aside.
2. Discard the water from the inner pot and return to the rice cooker. Press the white rice button to and add ½ teaspoon of oil and bacon. Cook until the bacon is browned but still tender. Remove from the inner cooking pot, add the chorizo and cook until all sides are brown. Place the bacon and chorizo on a plate to cool. Dice the bacon, slice the chorizo and set aside.
3. Drizzle oil or use cooking spray in the bottom of the inner pot to keep potatoes from sticking. Place the boiled potatoes in the inner cooking pot, cut side down and flatten with potato masher. Cook until the bottom part is browned, and then flip to brown the other side. Season to taste with salt and pepper.
4. Return the bacon and chorizo with the tomatoes to the inner pot and gently toss to combine. Crack the eggs and stir into the inner pot and add 2 tablespoons of water and close the lid. Cook for about 5 minutes, or until the egg whites are set and the yellow is still runny.
5. Adjust seasoning and switch to keep warm mode. Remove from the inner pot just before serving. Transfer to a serving plate, serve with avocado slices and parsley leaves on top.

SPANAKOPITA (GREEK SPINACH PIE)

I absolutely love spanakopita – the Greek spinach pie that is a staple on brunch menus – so you can imagine how delighted I was to find this recipe that's perfectly adapted for my rice cooker. If you're not familiar with this pastry-wrapped spinach-and-cheese deliciousness, all I can say is you're in for a treat. This is a wonderful dish to serve for breakfast, brunch, or an anytime snack when you really want to do your taste buds a favor.

Preparation time: 30 minutes

Cooking time: 1 hour

Yields: 5

INGREDIENTS:

2 tablespoons olive oil

1 medium onion, diced

¼ cup chopped green onions

2 garlic cloves, minced

2 cups tightly packed spinach, roughly chopped

½ cup loosely packed fresh parsley, chopped

2 whole eggs, beaten

½ cup goat's cheese

1 cup Feta cheese, crumbled

8 sheets phyllo dough

Olive oil, as needed for brushing dough

DIRECTIONS:

1. Place the inner cooking pot in the rice cooker, turn on and press the white rice button to start cooking. Add and heat the oil in the inner pot, sauté the garlic, onion, and green onions until soft and fragrant. Add parsley and spinach to the pot and cook for about 3 minutes, or until the spinach is wilted. Remove from the inner pot and set aside.
2. Combine together the goat's cheese, feta cheese and eggs in a mixing bowl and mix in the cooked spinach. Mix the ingredients and set aside.
3. Place one sheet of phyllo dough in the greased inner cooking pot, lightly brush with oil and cover with another sheet. Lightly brush the added phyllo dough and add with another sheet of dough. Lightly brush again with oil and add 1 more sheet.
4. Add the spinach mixture on the sheets of phyllo dough and spread evenly with a spatula. Repeat the process in adding sheets of phyllo dough on top of the spinach mixture.
5. Seal and join the edges with your fingers and place the inner cooking pot in the rice cooker. Close lid and cook for about 40 to 45 minutes, or until the bottom is browned. Switch to keep warm mode and remove from the inner cooking pot just before serving.
6. Remove the spinach pie from the inner pot, cut into wedges or squares then serve.

ITALIAN-FRENCH TOAST

Ok, we're all familiar with classic French toast, but this fantastic ricotta-and-parmesan laced recipe for Italian-French toast truly is a unique treat worth trying. This toast is more savory compared to the traditionally sweet French toast, and I love the way the seasonings and cheeses perfectly bring out the spinach and garlic in the mix. If you're looking for an elegant and original dish to serve at a family brunch or festive gathering, this recipe will work great. All my friends, family and guests love this Italian-French toast, and I know yours will too.

Preparation time: 15 minutes

Cooking time: 35 to 40 minutes

Yields: 4

INGREDIENTS:

For filling

1 tablespoons olive oil

1 garlic cloves, minced

1 cup tightly packed baby spinach

½ cup ricotta cheese

¼ cup Parmigiano-Reggiano cheese, grated

½ teaspoon of lemon zest, freshly grated

¼ cup loosely packed fresh basil leaves

¼ cup loosely packed fresh oregano leaves

Salt, to taste

Coarsely ground black pepper, to taste

For the toast

4 1-inch thick slices of French bread

2 medium whole eggs

½ cup whole milk

¼ teaspoon of salt

¼ teaspoon of garlic powder

1 tablespoon olive oil

1 cup of preferred marinara sauce, for serving

DIRECTIONS:

1. Place the inner cooking pot in the rice cooker, turn on and press the white rice button to start cooking. Add and heat the oil in the inner pot, add the garlic and sauté until brown and fragrant. Stir in the spinach and cook for about 4 to 5 minutes, or until the spinach is wilted while stirring occasionally. Remove spinach from the inner cooking pot and place in a bowl.
2. Mix in the grated Parmigiano-Reggiano, ricotta, zest of lemon, oregano and basil in with the spinach mixture while stirring the ingredients until well combined. Season to taste with salt and pepper. Set aside.
3. Make a shallow horizontal incision to form a pocket on each slice of bread. Carefully stuff each pocket with spinach-cheese mixture, and then gently press with your thumb and finger to close. Repeat the procedure with the remaining slices of breads.
4. In a shallow dish, add the milk, eggs, garlic powder and salt and whisk thoroughly.
5. Return the inner cooking pot in the rice cooker and press the white rice button to cook. Add a tablespoon of oil to the inner cooking pot and wait until hot. Dip the bread slices in the egg

mixture and coat evenly on all sides. Place 2 slices in the rice cooker and cook until golden brown. Turn to cook the other side until both sides are evenly brown. Cook remaining bread slices.

6. Return the cooked bread slice to the inner pot and switch to keep warm mode. Remove from the inner pot just before serving.

7. Portion onto individual serving plates, serve warm with marinara sauce on top or on the side.

MASHED POTATO PANCAKES

I love a good potato pancake, and I particularly love how easy and fast they are to prepare in my rice-cooker. This recipe keeps the flavors simple, balanced, and delicious, with finely diced white onion and just a pinch of salt and pepper adding a wonderful savory layer to that potato-pancake goodness. These are a wonderful dish to serve at breakfast or brunch, or even lunch or dinner. Let's face it, there's no wrong time to enjoy a potato pancake – and I guarantee these will hit the spot no matter when you serve them.

Preparation time: 20 minutes

Cooking time: 30 to 40 minutes

Yields: 4

INGREDIENTS:

1 cup mashed potatoes

2 small whole eggs, beaten in separate bowls

1 small onion, finely diced

Pinch of salt and black pepper, to taste

Flour, sifted for dredging

½ cup bread crumbs

2 tablespoons cooking oil, for frying

DIRECTIONS:

1. Combine together the mashed potatoes, one egg, onion and season to taste with salt and pepper. Mix the ingredients until well combined and divide into 8 equal portions.
2. Flatten each portion with both hands to form into patties. Dredge the patties in a bowl with flour, coat with beaten egg and then with bread crumbs. Place it on a plate, set aside.

3. Place the inner cooking pot in the rice cooker, turn on and press the white rice button to start cooking. Add the oil and heat it until smoking, place the patties in the inner cooking pot and cook until the bottom part is nicely browned. Turn to cook the other side, close lid and switch to keep warm mode. Remove patties from the inner pot just before serving. You may need to cook the patties in separate batches to fit in the inner cooking pot.
4. Remove the patties from the inner pot, transfer to as serving plate and serve warm.

Cinnamon Apple Oatmeal

Forget the notion that oatmeal is a "boring" – albeit healthy – breakfast choice. With a little cinnamon, coconut milk, almond extract and chopped apple, the classic breakfast staple gets a delicious sweet makeover that is anything but boring. This is a great breakfast to serve when you want to start the day off on the best possible foot; this oatmeal will be a hit with your family, and will stick to their ribs to boot!

Preparation time: 5 minutes

Cooking time: 30 to 40 minutes

Yields: 3 to 4

INGREDIENTS:

1 cup steel cut oats

1 teaspoon cinnamon powder

pinch of salt

1 cup coconut milk

½ cup water, or as needed

½ teaspoon almond extract

2 to 3 tablespoons of local honey

1 apple, core removed and finely chopped

DIRECTIONS:

1. Add the oats, coconut milk, water, almond extract, 2 tablespoons of honey, cinnamon and salt in the inner cooking pot. Briefly stir to combine.
2. Place the inner cooking pot in the rice cooker, turn on and press the white rice button to start cooking. Close lid and cook until the oats have absorbed most of the liquids. Stir in the apple and

add the remaining honey if needed. Adjust consistency according to preference by adding more water and cook until the desired consistency is achieved.

3. Switch to keep warm mode, let it stand for 10 minutes in the inner cooking pot to thicken.
4. Remove the inner cooking pot from the rice cooker. Portion oatmeal into individual serving bowls and serve warm.

Philly Scrapple

This classic down-home recipe is a favorite far outside its birthplace of Philadelphia, and it's not hard to understand why. The marjoram, nutmeg and garlic in the recipe perfectly season the pork, and the touch of basil lends an earthy flavor that makes this an ideal meal to serve in the winter months. There is no better way to start the day than with a hearty serving of this scrapple, so whip up a batch and give your family a breakfast that will power them through the morning!

Preparation time: 30 minutes

Cooking time: 60 minutes

Yields: 3 to 4

INGREDIENTS:

1 pound of lean ground pork

1 cup cornmeal

1 tablespoon fresh basil leaves

1 tablespoon sage

½ tablespoon salt

¼ tablespoon garlic powder

¼ tablespoon marjoram

1 teaspoon black pepper

½ tablespoon nutmeg

¼ tablespoon onion powder

DIRECTIONS:

1. Place the ground pork in the inner cooking pot and fill with water just to cover the meat. Place the inner cooking pot in the rice cooker, turn on and press the white rice button to start cooking. Boil the ground meat until it turns to grey in color and the liquid has reduced.
2. Pour the pot contents on a large bowl with a strainer on top. Set the meat in the strainer to the side. Reserve about half of the cooking liquid and return to the inner cooking pot. Press the white rice button and bring the cooking liquid to a boil. Gradually add in the cornmeal while stirring constantly to avoid lumps to form in the mixture. Return the ground meat to the inner cooking pot and cook for 30 minutes while stirring occasionally.
3. Stir in the seasonings and cook for another 2 minutes, or until well incorporated while stirring regularly. Remove the inner cooking pot from the rice cooker and let it rest to lower in temperature.
4. When the mixture has lowered in temperature, pour into a loaf pan and chill for at least 3 hours before serving.
5. Slice the chilled scrapple and fry before serving.

Cajun-Style Shrimp and Grits

If you like shrimp and if you like grits – or even if you're unfamiliar with both! – you'll love this recipe for Cajun-seasoned shrimp and grits. The andouille sausage in this recipe really kicks the flavors up a notch, and helps cook the shrimp and the grits in the savory natural oils. Feel free to adjust the seasonings in this recipe according to taste – I like mine quite spicy, and my family seems to agree, but this dish will work equally well with less pepper or even none at all for milder palates.

Preparation time: 15 minutes

Cooking time: 1 hour to 1 hour 30 minutes

Yields: 6

INGREDIENTS:

2 cups regular grits

1 to 1 ½ cups chicken stock

3 cups water

3 to 4 links of Cajun Style Andouille, casings removed and diced

1 teaspoon salt

1 teaspoon black pepper, coarsely ground

2 cups of raw fresh shrimp, peeled and deveined

2 to 3 teaspoons Cajun seasoning

½ cup unsalted butter

1 cup white cheddar cheese, shredded

½ cup loosely packed fresh green onion, chopped

DIRECTIONS:

1. Place the grits, Cajun sausage, stock, water, salt and pepper in the inner cooking pot. Place inner pot in the rice cooker, turn on and press the white rice button to start cooking.
2. Season shrimp with the Cajun spice mix and mix it well with hands to evenly coat the shrimp. Place the coated shrimp on a steamer basket and place it on top of the inner cooking pot. Close the lid cook for about 1 hour to 1 hour and 30 minutes, or until the shrimp and grits are cooked through.
3. Remove the steamer basket with the shrimp, transfer the shrimp in a large bowl and stir in the butter, green onions and the cheese. Melt the butter completely before serving.
4. Portion grits on individual serving plates or bowls. Serve warm with shrimp on top.

Tex-Mex Migas

This fantastic southwestern-style scramble, laden with veggies and cheese and corn tortillas, makes an awesome breakfast, brunch, or lunch. This preparation comes with a delicious sweet-and-spicy bite thanks to the jalapeño and garlic mingling with that delicious mango salsa, and the avocados in the mix tie in all the flavors with their unmistakable creamy goodness. This is a wonderful dish to serve at a family gathering or on special occasions – perfect for sharing, this is a truly festive and hearty feast. Enjoy!

Preparation time: 10 minutes

Cooking time: 25 to 30 minutes

Yields: 4 to 6

INGREDIENTS:

5 whole eggs

2 tablespoons butter

1 teaspoon milk

¼ cup jalapeño, chopped

1 small onion, diced

1 tomato, diced

1 garlic clove, crushed

4 corn tortilla

½ cup Monterey Jack cheese, shredded

Hot chili sauce, for serving

1 avocado, pitted and halved lengthwise, cut on the bias

Mango salsa, for serving

Salt, to taste

DIRECTIONS:

1. Place the inner cooking pot in the rice cooker, turn on and press the white rice button to start cooking. Melt the butter in the cooking pot then add the garlic and sauté with onions until soft and lightly brown. Stir in the tomatoes and jalapeño, close lid and cook until soft and cooked through.
2. Tear tortillas into small pieces add it in the inner cooking pot.
3. Whisk the eggs, 1 teaspoon milk, cheese and a pinch of salt in a mixing bowl. Pour it in the inner cooking pot, briefly mix to combine. Close the lid and cook for 2 minutes, or until the eggs are set. Switch to keep warm mode, stir and let it cook for 10 minutes with low heat.
4. Remove from the inner cooking pot and transfer to a serving plate. Serve warm with avocado slices, mango salsa and hot sauce.

7

VEGETABLE AND SIDE DISH RECIPES

WILTED SPINACH

I really love this preparation for wilted spinach, which takes the staple vegetable up a notch with a touch of sugar, a healthy dose of tangy onions and a little lemon juice, and just enough salt and pepper to create a truly delectable side-dish. Everyone knows that spinach is incredibly healthy – but only a few of us know how delicious it can be. Try this awesome recipe, and you'll see just what I mean.

Preparation time: 10 minutes

Cooking time: 30 minutes

Yields: 4 to 6

INGREDIENTS:

½ cup bacon, cooked and crumbled

2 medium onions, diced

2 tablespoons sugar

1 lemon, juiced

½ teaspoon salt

Freshly ground black pepper, to taste

4 cups loosely packed fresh spinach leaves, torn

DIRECTIONS:

1. Place the inner cooking pot in the rice cooker, turn on and press the white rice button to start cooking. Add the bacon in the inner cooking pot and cook until crisp and brown. Remove from the inner pot with a slotted spoon, transfer to a plate and set aside.
2. In the inner pot with bacon fat, add the onions, sugar, lemon juice, and then season to taste with salt and pepper. Stir the ingredients regularly and cook for 10 minutes, or until the onions are soft.

3. Stir in the spinach, close lid and cook for about 5 minutes or until the spinach is wilted. Open lid and stir in half of the crumbled bacon, switch to keep warm mode and cook for 5 minutes with low heat. Remove the inner cooking pot from the rice cooker.
4. Portion spinach onto individual serving dishes, top with the remaining bacon and drizzle with extra lemon juice. Serve immediately.

Steamed Artichokes

Steamed artichokes are quite simple to steam in the rice cooker. This recipe includes fennel, parsley, shallots and capers, along with an anchovy filet and a touch of cream, for a truly delectable artichoke dish that couldn't be easier to prepare. This is a wonderfully sophisticated dish to serve at an elegant party or gathering, both scrumptious and unique, so serve it with pride and make sure to get a helping for yourself before it's all gone!

Preparation time: 15 minutes

Cooking time: 30 minutes

Yields: 4

INGREDIENTS:

½ teaspoon of toasted fennel seeds

½ cup loosely packed fresh parsley leaves

3 tablespoons drained capers, rinsed

2 shallots, chopped

2 garlic cloves, minced

2 tablespoons fresh tarragon leaves

1 anchovy fillet

½ teaspoon crushed red pepper flakes

½ cup olive oil

3 tablespoons of whipping cream

1 tablespoon Sherry vinegar

4 large globe artichokes, trimmed

½ lemon, juiced

DIRECTIONS:

1. In a skillet over medium-high heat, toast the fennel seeds for about 2 minutes, or until aromatic. Remove from heat and transfer to a food processor, together with the capers, shallot, parsley, garlic, tarragon, pepper flakes and the anchovy. Pulse until a coarse mixture is achieved while scraping the sides regularly. Transfer the mixture to a bowl and add the vinegar, oil and cream. Season with salt and pepper and whisk the ingredients thoroughly until well incorporated. Cover bowl and set aside.
2. Rub the artichokes evenly with lemon juice on all sides and lightly squeeze to release the juice. Transfer into the inner cooking pot and pour in 2 cups of water. Place the inner cooking pot in the rice cooker, turn on and press the white rice button to start cooking. Cook for about 20 minutes or until the artichokes are tender and cooked through. Switch to keep warm mode, and cook for 10 minutes with low heat. Remove the inner cooking pot from the rice cooker.
3. Place one artichoke each serving dishes, portion the Salsa Verde into four serving bowls. Serve.

STEAMED BROCCOLI WITH BACON

If you're looking for a way to make healthy-healthy broccoli into a truly tempting dish, look no further than this scrumptious recipe for broccoli and bacon. The salty bacon cooks up perfectly with the broccoli and the cauliflower alike, infusing the vegetables with that unmistakable smoky bacon flavor, and the touch of lemon helps marry all the flavors together. This side-dish is as nutritious as it is delicious, and really a wonderful way to get everyone excited about their cruciferous vegetables, so give it a try and get ready to fall in love with the power-combo of broccoli and bacon!

Preparation time: 5 minutes

Cooking time: 15 minutes

Yields: 4

INGREDIENTS:

1 medium head of broccoli, detached florets

1 medium head of cauliflower, detached florets

Pinch of salt and pepper, to taste

2 cups water, or as needed

1 tablespoon minced parsley, for serving

Crispy bacon bits, for serving

1 tablespoon lemon juice, for serving (optional)

DIRECTIONS:

1. Wash and drain the cauliflower and broccoli, cut into individual florets. Place vegetables on a steam tray and add 2 cups of water in the inner cooking pot, or as needed to cover. Place the inner cooking pot in the rice cooker and the steam tray on top over the inner cooking pot. Close the lid, turn on and press the white rice button to start cooking. Steam the vegetables for about 8 to 10

minutes, or until soft but still crisp. Switch to keep warm mode and cook further for 5 minutes with low heat.

2. Remove the steam tray with a mitt or cloth. Carefully remove the vegetables and transfer to a serving plate. Season to taste with salt and pepper and drizzle with lemon juice on top. Serve warm with crispy bacon bits on top.

COLLARD GREENS

Collard greens are a staple of the American South, and have since become increasingly popular in the rest of the U.S. as well. It's not hard to see why, and this recipe perfectly highlights the crisp, earthy flavor of the greens with a touch of onion and garlic, and just enough chicken stock and red pepper flakes to make every bite perfectly savory and spicy. These greens are a wonderfully nutritious addition to any meal, and they're absolutely scrumptious to boot – so serve up a batch today, and be prepared for everyone to ask for a second-helping!

Preparation time: 10 minutes

Cooking time: 1 hour

Yields: 4

INGREDIENTS:

1 tablespoon of extra virgin olive oil

4 slices of bacon, chopped

1 medium onion, diced

2 garlic cloves, minced

½ teaspoon salt or as needed, to taste

½ teaspoon black pepper, freshly ground

3 cups chicken stock

¼ teaspoon crushed red pepper flakes

2 stems spring onions, chopped

2 cups of tightly packed fresh collard greens, roughly chopped

DIRECTIONS:

1. Place the inner cooking pot in the rice cooker, turn on and press the white rice button to start cooking. When the inner pot is hot, add the bacon and cook until crisp. Remove with a slotted spoon and transfer into a plate. Let it rest to cool and finely chop.
2. Add the onions to the inner cooking pot and sauté until soft and translucent using bacon fat. Stir in the garlic and cook for 2 to 3 minutes, or until lightly brown and fragrant while stirring regularly. Stir in the collard greens and cook for 5 minutes, or until wilted while stirring occasionally.
3. Add the chicken stock and season to taste with salt, pepper and crushed pepper flakes. Cover lid and bring to a boil. Cook for 30 minutes and switch to keep warm mode. Maintain keep warm mode for 15 minutes to finish the cooking process with low heat. Remove the inner cooking pot from the rice cooker.
4. Portion greens into individual serving bowls and ladle in the soup. Serve warm with extra pepper flakes and spring onions on top.

Butter Mushrooms with Beer

This mushroom recipe is exactly as delicious as it sounds – and don't worry, it's plenty "safe" for kids and for those who prefer no alcohol as the alcohol in the beer all cooks off. If you like mushrooms as I do, and always find yourself looking for new and interesting preparations, don't miss this delicious and unique dish that's sure to be a hit with all your friends, family, and guests.

Preparation time: 5 minutes

Cooking time: 30 minutes

Serves: 6

INGREDIENTS:

4 cups of canned button mushrooms, rinsed and drained

¼ cup of butter

1 cup of beer

2 tablespoons of fresh parsley leaves, chopped

1 teaspoon dried thyme

Salt and coarsely ground black pepper, to taste

DIRECTIONS:

1. Place the inner cooking pot in the rice cooker, turn on and press the white rice button to start cooking. Melt in the butter in the inner pot and add the button mushrooms. Gently toss to coat the mushrooms with butter and cook for 3 minutes.
2. Pour in the beer in the inner cooking pot, cover lid and bring to a boil. Cook for 10 minutes and then switch to keep warm mode. Stir in the thyme, 1 tablespoon of parsley and season to taste with salt and pepper. Close lid, stir occasionally and maintain

keep warm mode for 20 minutes. Remove the inner cooking pot from the rice cooker.

3. Portion the mushrooms onto individual serving plates, serve warm with extra parsley leaves on top.

Steamed Japanese Yam Curry with Lime

This amazing vegetarian curry dish is an awesome appetizer or side-plate for any meal. The sweetness of the yams combined with tangy cilantro and lime, plus lightly spicy curry powder and the nutty twist of sesame oil, is truly a taste sensation. My whole family is delighted when I whip up this delicious curry, and I know yours will love it, too. Best of all, it couldn't be easier to prepare with a good rice-cooker, so get on it and serve with pride!

Preparation time: 10 minutes

Cooking time: 20 minutes

Yields: 4

INGREDIENTS:

4 to 6 small Japanese yams, quartered

1 tablespoon of fresh cilantro, chopped

1 tablespoon of lime juice

1 tablespoon toasted sesame oil

1 teaspoon of curry powder

¼ teaspoon salt, to taste

DIRECTIONS:

1. Add 2 cups of water in the inner cooking pot and place it in the rice cooker. Turn on and press the white rice button to start cooking. Place the yams on the steam tray and place it in the inner cooking pot. Close lid and bring the water to a boil. Steam for about 15 to 20 minutes, or until the yams are tender with a fork.
2. While steaming the yams, whisk together the lime juice, sesame oil and curry powder in a small bowl until well incorporated. Set aside.

3. Once the yams are done, transfer to a bowl and top with cilantro. Pour in the lime and oil mixture and gently toss to coat the yams evenly with the flavoring ingredients.

4. Serve warm.

SAUTEED WATERCRESS AND BOK CHOY

This delicious vegetable side comes loaded with nutritious yet delicate fresh greens. I love the combination of the watercress and bok choy together – slightly spicy, and perfectly complementary – given an extra flavor kick with garlic and toasted sesame seeds. This is a terrific side-dish to serve with any meal, and a wonderful way to get a dose of leafy green vegetables that is both unique and scrumptious.

Preparation time: 5 minutes

Cooking time: 10 minutes

Serves: 2-3

INGREDIENTS:

1 tablespoon olive oil

2 to 3 garlic cloves, peeled and thinly sliced

½ pound watercress, chopped

1 cup loosely packed baby Bok Choy, trimmed and chopped

Salt and ground, to taste

¼ cup chicken stock or water

1 to 2 teaspoons of toasted sesame seeds

DIRECTIONS:

Place the inner cooking pot in the rice cooker, turn on and press the white rice button to start cooking. Add and heat the olive oil, sauté in the garlic for 1 minute while stirring regularly. Stir in the Bok Choy and watercress, season to taste with salt and pepper. Pour in the stock, cover lid and bring to a boil. Cook for 4 to 6 minutes or until the vegetables are wilted, switch to keep warm mode and stir in the toasted sesame seeds. Serve with extra toasted sesame seeds on top.

Chili Scallops with Baby Bok Choy

If you're not used to cooking with sea scallops, there's no need to be afraid! This recipe, which will work with any well-made rice cooker, is basically foolproof, and 100% delicious. The mix of herbs and spices in this tangy blend is the perfect flavor complement to those delectable scallops, and the bok choy in the mix ensures that this is a complete and nutritious dish, even if you serve it by itself.

Preparation time: 5 minutes

Cooking time: 15 minutes

Yields: 3 to 4

INGREDIENTS:

1 ½ cups fresh sea scallops, rinsed and pat dried, thinly sliced

¼ cup chicken stock

1 tablespoon chili bean sauce

1 tablespoon light soy sauce

½ tablespoon cornstarch

2 tablespoons peanut oil

1 tablespoon of minced ginger

3 garlic cloves, minced

½ teaspoon salt

1 scallion, chopped

8 small heads of baby Bok Choy, base trimmed and chopped

1 medium red bell pepper, seeded and cut into strips

Diced scallions (for serving)

DIRECTIONS:

1. Combine together the stock, soy sauce, chili bean paste, and cornstarch in a bowl and set aside.
2. Place the inner cooking pot in the rice cooker, turn on and press the white rice button to start cooking. Add half the peanut oil, sauté the garlic and ginger for 1 minute, or until lightly brown and aromatic. Add the scallops and arrange them in an even layer. Cook undisturbed for 1 minute, season to taste with salt and cook for another minute while stirring regularly.
3. Once the scallops are opaque but not yet fully cooked, remove and transfer to a plate. Set aside.
4. Add the remaining peanut oil in the inner cooking pot, and then add the bell pepper and Bok Choy and season with salt to taste. Cook for 2 minutes while tossing the ingredients. Return the scallops and pour in the stock mixture. Briefly stir and cover with the lid, bringing to a boil. Switch to keep warm mode and wait for 10 minutes to cook further with low heat. Remove the inner cooking pot from the rice cooker.
5. Portion the scallops and Bok Choy into individual serving bowls, serve immediately with scallions on top.

PEPPERED SHRIMP

Shrimp is such a wonderful source of lean protein, and with this sweet-and-spicy peppered rub they truly get the flavor treatment they deserve. I love the garlic and ginger root in this recipe, which add amazing flavor while cooking. These shrimp are a perfect dish to serve as an elegant appetizer or main course at a sophisticated dinner party. Be prepared to impress everyone with this awesome peppered seafood goodness!

Preparation time: 15 minutes

Cooking time: 15 minutes

Yields: 4

INGREDIENTS:

½ teaspoon of salt

2 cups fresh shrimp, rinsed and drained, peeled and deveined

½ teaspoon sugar

½ teaspoon Szechuan peppercorns, crushed

1 tablespoon peanut oil

3 garlic cloves, minced

1-inch fresh ginger root, minced

1 jalapeno chili, diced

DIRECTIONS:

1. Pat shrimp dry with paper towels. Set aside.
2. Combine together sugar, ½ teaspoon salt, and crushed Szechuan peppercorns in a mixing bowl. Set aside.
3. Place the inner cooking pot in the rice cooker, turn on and press the white rice button to start cooking. Add and heat the oil, sauté the garlic, ginger and jalapeno until fragrant. Add the shrimp and

arrange them in an even layer, cook for 2 minute without stirring.

4. Switch to keep warm mode and stir in the seasoning mixture. Close lid and cook for 10 minutes with low heat. Open lid and briefly stir the ingredients. Remove the inner cooking pot from heat.

5. Transfer to a serving dish and serve immediately with extra crushed peppers on top.

Steamed Asian Dumplings

Who doesn't love steamed pork dumplings? I know they're my absolute favorite item on an Asian takeout menu – but what I love even better is this recipe that I've developed to make right in my own kitchen, in the rice-cooker! It's not quite as effortless as ordering in takeout, but it's pretty darn painless, and boy are the results delicious. Hot, fresh, and perfectly seasoned, these dumplings are a good enough reason to lose those takeout menus forever!

Preparation time: 30 minutes

Cooking time: 20 minutes

Yields: 8 to 10

INGREDIENTS:

20 to 30 wonton wrappers

Soy dipping sauce, for serving

Limes, halved for serving

1 cup water

For the stuffing

1 cup ground pork

2 scallions, chopped

¼ cup loosely packed fresh cilantro, chopped

2 tablespoons light soy sauce

2 garlic cloves, minced

1 tablespoon of rice vinegar

1-inch fresh ginger root, minced

1 teaspoon sesame oil

½ tablespoon sugar

½ head of cabbage leaves, thinly sliced

½ tablespoon black pepper, freshly ground

1 egg white

DIRECTIONS:

1. In a large mixing bowl, combine together all ingredients for the stuffing until well incorporated. Place one wrapper on your palm and add 1 tablespoon of pork mixture. Lightly wet the edges of the wrapper and with your fingers, join the wet edges to secure the stuffing. Repeat the procedure with the remaining ingredients.
2. Add 1 cup of water in the inner cooking pot and place into the rice cooker, turn on and press the white rice button to start cooking. Bring the water to a boil.
3. Place the dumplings on the greased steam tray and place it in the inner cooking pot. Close the lid and steam the dumplings for 15 to 20 minutes. Switch to keep warm mode and let the dumplings stay warm before serving.
4. Serve the steamed pork dumplings with soy dipping sauce and limes.

Falafel Cake with Cucumber-Yogurt Dressing over Pita

This amazing single-dish rendition of classic Israeli falafel is one of my all-time favorite side-dishes – so much that I often serve it as a standalone centerpiece meal! This nutritious and delicious seasoned chickpea creation is a great choice to serve at a party or family gathering festive and irresistible, and perfect for sharing! It couldn't be easier or faster to prepare with a good rice-cooker, so give it a try today, and enjoy!

Preparation time: 10 minutes

Cooking time: 20 minutes

Serves: 4

INGREDIENTS:

2 tablespoons of olive oil

2 pita breads, cut into 2 portions each

1 cup loosely packed fresh arugula

1 cup of cucumber-yogurt dressing

For the falafel

1 red onion, minced

2 tablespoons Dijon mustard

½ tablespoon cumin powder

½ tablespoon paprika

¼ teaspoon black pepper, freshly ground

¼ teaspoon salt

1 cup canned chickpeas, rinsed and drained

1 thick slice of whole wheat bread, torn into small pieces

1 whole egg

1 egg white

DIRECTIONS:

1. In a large food processor, combine together all ingredients for the falafel and pulse until a coarse texture of mixture is achieved. Transfer mixture to a bowl and set aside.
2. Place the inner cooking pot in the rice cooker, turn on and press the white rice button to start cooking. Add and heat the oil until smoking, add in the chickpea mixture and close the lid. Cook for 10 minutes, or until the bottom is lightly brown and crispy. Turn the cake to cook the other side for another 10 minutes, close lid. Remove the inner cooking pot from the rice cooker. Place the cake on a plate, set aside to cool and divide into 4 slices.
3. Place the halved pitas on a work surface and put a bed of arugula on top. Place a slice of falafel over the arugula and spoon over with cucumber-yogurt on each slice of falafel. Serve immediately.

Syrian Green Beans with Olive Oil

If you want a vegetable side-dish with a twist, I highly recommend these delicious Syrian-style seasoned green beans. The touch of garlic and cilantro in this recipe gives them the perfect flavor balance between tangy and spicy, and they go great as an appetizer or accompaniment to all sorts of dishes. Feel free to serve with or without the pita bread, as desired – they're great either way, and will be a huge hit with your friends, family, or guests!

Preparation time: 5 minutes

Cooking time: 25 minutes

Yields: 4

INGREDIENTS:

1 pound green beans

Black pepper, to taste

¼ cup olive oil

¼ teaspoon salt, to taste

2 garlic clove, minced

¼ cup loosely packed fresh cilantro, chopped

2 pita rounds, torn or sliced into pieces

DIRECTIONS:

1. Add the beans in the inner cooking pot, drizzle with olive oil and season to taste with salt and pepper. Place the inner cooking pot in the rice cooker, turn on and press the white rice button to start cooking. Stir the ingredients briefly, close the lid and cook for 15 to 20 minutes, or until tender and cooked through.
2. Open lid and stir in the garlic and cilantro. Cook for 2 minutes, or until the cilantro are wilted. Remove the inner cooking pot from the rice cooker. Serve warm with pita slices.

OKRA MASALA

Okra is rightly known as a "wonder-food," packed with nutrients and anti-oxidants, and in this delicious recipe it gets a perfect flavor treatment with masala spices and seasonings, kicked up with juicy tomatoes and onions. This side-dish is your best bet if you want to serve up vegetables that are truly as good for the body as they are for the taste-buds. Eat happy, eat healthy, and get some of this okra on the table today!

Preparation time: 20 minutes

Cooking time: 25 minutes

Yields: 3 to 4

INGREDIENTS

1 cup okra, base trimmed, rinsed and dried, cut into 1-inch pieces

1 red onion, diced

2 ripe red tomatoes, diced

1 teaspoon of minced fresh ginger root and 3 garlic cloves in a paste mixture

1 teaspoon coriander powder

½ teaspoon of red hot chili powder

½ teaspoon of turmeric powder

½ teaspoon garam masala

½ teaspoon dry mango powder

Salt, as needed to taste

2 tablespoons of oil, for frying the okra

1 tablespoon oil, for the onion-tomato masala

1 teaspoon crushed dry fenugreek leaves crushed (optional)

DIRECTIONS:

1. Place the inner cooking pot in the rice cooker, turn on and press the white rice button to start cooking. Add the 2 tablespoons of oil and heat until smoking, and add the okra and cook until soft, stirring occasionally. Remove from the inner cooking pot, transfer to a plate and set aside.
2. Add 1 tablespoon of oil in the inner cooking pot and sauté the onions until soft and translucent. Stir in the garlic-ginger paste and sauté for 1 minute, or until aromatic. Add the diced tomatoes and cook until tender.
3. Stir in the dried spices one at a time and stir to combine. Close lid and cook for 10 minutes. Return the okra, crushed fenugreek, and salt in the inner cooking pot. Stir to coat the okra with the spice mixture, close lid and switch to keep warm mode. Maintain in keep warm mode until serving the okra masala.
4. Transfer into individual serving bowls or dishes, serve warm with chopped cilantro and flat breads.

Polish Stuffed Cabbage Recipe

This stuffed-cabbage recipe has been in my family for generations – the story goes that a great-great-great aunt of mine actually brought it over with her from Warsaw. But it's only recently that I started preparing it in my rice cooker, and I have to say the results are phenomenal. The dish is every bit as scrumptious, but takes a fraction of the time and trouble as the traditional preparation! I have no doubt that my Polish ancestor would be nothing but proud of this amazing dish – and then ask for second-helpings, as everyone always does when I whip up a batch of this stuffed-cabbage.

Preparation time: 30 minutes

Cooking time: 3 hours 30 minutes

Yields: 6 to 8

INGREDIENTS:

1 large head of cabbage, leaves separated

1 cup cooked long -grain white rice

1 large whole egg, beaten

¼ cup fresh milk

2 medium onions, diced

2 cups ground beef, browned

½ tablespoon salt

½ tablespoon black pepper

1 cup canned tomato sauce

1 to 2 tablespoons brown sugar

1 lemon, juiced

1 tablespoon of Worcestershire sauce

DIRECTIONS:

1. Add 2 cups of water into the inner cooking pot, place inner pot into the rice cooker. Turn on and press the white rice button to start cooking. Bring water to a boil and blanch the cabbage leaves for 2 minutes. Remove from the inner cooking pot and transfer to a bowl with an ice bath.
2. Combine together the rice, beaten egg, beef, milk and onion in a mixing bowl. Season to taste with salt and pepper, and then mix to combine.
3. Place the cabbage leaves on a work surface. Add ¼ cup of beef mixture on the center, fold the sides and roll the leaves upward. Repeat the procedure with the remaining ingredients. Place the cabbage rolls in the inner cooking pot. You may arrange them in two layers to fit in the inner pot.
4. Whisk together the tomato sauce, lemon juice, sugar and the Worcestershire sauce in mixing bowl until the sugar is completely dissolved. Pour it in the inner cooking pot with the cabbage rolls. Close lid and cook for 20 minutes. Switch to keep warm mode and cook for another 3 hours with low heat.
5. Carefully transfer the cabbage rolls to a serving dish and serve with sauce on top.

Carrots and Lentils

It's wonderfully easy to turn carrots and lentils into a nutritious dish with the help of your rice cooker and a few seasonings. If you're cooking for strict vegetarians, feel free to substitute the chicken stock for vegetable stock, and to just add extra parsley instead of the bacon bits to make this truly herbivore-friendly (and every bit as yummy). It's hard to mess up this scrumptious and healthy dish, so have at it and enjoy!

Preparation time: 10 minutes

Cooking time: 20 to 25 minutes

Yields: 3 to 4

INGREDIENTS:

3 garlic cloves, minced

1 cup lentils

1 large carrot, peeled and cut into sticks

¼ cup chicken stock

1 tablespoon of olive oil

Salt and pepper, to taste

2 tablespoons crispy bacon bits

1 tablespoon of chopped parsley

DIRECTIONS:

1. Place the inner cooking pot in the rice cooker, turn on and press the white rice button to start cooking. Add the oil and sauté the garlic until lightly brown and aromatic.
2. Add the lentils and carrots in the inner pot and cook for 2 minutes while stirring regularly. Pour in ½ cup stock and season to taste with salt and pepper. Close lid and bring to a boil. Switch

to keep warm mode and let it cook with low heat for 10 minutes. Remove the inner cooking pot from the rice cooker.

3. Portion vegetables into individual serving bowls and serve warm with crispy bacon bits and parsley leaves on top.

ITALIAN-STYLE SWISS CHARD FRITTATA

This frittata works great as a side-dish, but to be honest I've served it up before as its own meal and gotten nothing but rave reviews. Filled with nutritious Swiss chard, tangy red onions, and just enough cheese and seasonings to make every bite a savory taste delight, this frittata is an elegant and crowd-pleasing addition to any meal.

Preparation time: 10 minutes

Cooking time: 30 minutes

Yields: 4

INGREDIENTS:

6 large whole eggs

¼ teaspoon salt, to taste

½ teaspoon freshly cracked black pepper

1 cup Swiss chard, trimmed and blanched

1 tablespoon of olive oil

1 ripe red onion, diced

1 teaspoon dried basil leaves

1 cup grated Pecorino Romano cheese

DIRECTIONS:

1. Whisk the eggs in a mixing bowl until foamy. Stir in the Swiss chard, cheese, salt and cracked black pepper.
2. Place the inner cooking pot in the rice cooker, turn on and press the white rice button to start cooking. Add the oil and saute the onions until soft. Pour in the egg mixture, stir briefly and close the lid, cooking for about 6 to 8 minutes. Gently lift the frittata to allow the uncooked mixture to drizzle down and close lid, switch

to keep warm mode and cook for 15 to 20 minutes, or until the eggs are set and cooked through.

3. Remove the inner cooking pot from the rice cooker. Place a plate on top and carefully turn it upside down to remove the frittata.
4. Serve immediately with extra basil leaves and grated cheese on top.

MEDITERRANEAN KALE

If you've relegated kale to the boring eat-it-because-you-have-to ultra-super-healthy-but-tasteless food pile, it's time to rethink it. This recipe for Mediterranean-style kale, with soy sauce and garlic and a wonderful savory lemon and olive oil base, is just what you need to make kale as delicious as it is nutritious. This is a great side dish to serve at any family dinner, and you'll love how easy it is to get kids – and adults! – to eat vegetables when they're this tasty.

Preparation time: 5 minutes

Cooking time: 10 minutes

Yields: 3 to 4

INGREDIENTS:

6 cups chopped kale

1 tablespoon lemon juice

1 tablespoon olive oil, or as needed

1 teaspoon minced garlic

1 teaspoon soy sauce

salt to taste

ground black pepper to taste

DIRECTIONS:

1. Add a cup of water to the inner cooking pot, and then place the inner cooking pot in the rice cooker. Turn on and press the white rice button to start cooking. Close the lid and bring to a boil.
2. Place the kale on the steam tray, place the steam tray in the inner cooking pot, close the lid and steam kale for 8 to 10 minutes.

3. While steaming the kale, whisk together the soy sauce, lemon juice, oil, garlic, salt and pepper in a mixing bowl until the salt is completely dissolved.

3. When the kale is done, remove from the rice cooker and transfer to the bowl to be topped with the dressing. Toss to coat and transfer to a serving dish. Serve warm.

CLASSIC GREEK SPINACH

The garlic, tomatoes, and savory chicken stock are what make this spinach dish truly special. We all know that spinach is an incredibly healthy ingredient, but it really gets the attention it deserves with these delicious seasonings that elevate it to scrumptious side-dish. This spinach will work great as an accompaniment to any meal, but particularly with Greek or Mediterranean-flavored dishes. However you serve it, get ready for a ton of compliments on this savory and nutritious dish!

Preparation time: 30 minutes

Cooking time: 40 hour

Yields: 4

INGREDIENTS:

1 cup of extra virgin olive oil

½ cup of diced onions

1 cup tightly packed spinach

2 medium ripe red tomatoes, diced

3 cups chicken stock, or as needed

1 garlic clove, minced

2 tablespoons of tomato paste

salt and pepper to taste

½ cup uncooked long-grain white rice, rinsed and drained

DIRECTIONS:

1. Place the inner cooking pot in the rice cooker, turn on and press the white rice button to start cooking. Add the oil and sauté the onion and garlic until soft fragrant. Stir in the spinach and tomatoes and cook until the spinach is wilted and the tomatoes are tender.
2. Pour in 2 cups of stock, season to taste with salt and pepper. Add the tomato paste, close the lid and cook for about 15 minutes.
3. Add the rice and remaining stock, close lid and cook for another 20 minutes, or until the rice is cooked through and fluffy.
4. Remove the inner cooking pot from the rice cooker. Transfer rice and spinach to individual serving bowls. Serve warm.

SAUTEED SWISS CHARD WITH PARMESAN CHEESE

Swiss chard is one of my all-time favorite vegetables – of course it's incredibly healthy, one of the best of the leafy-green options, but it's also simply scrumptious when lightly sautéed with a touch of parmesan cheese. This recipe for that irresistible dish is an excellent choice for elegant dinner parties, when you want a side-dish to truly set a sophisticated tone for the rest of the meal.

Preparation time: 10 minutes

Cooking time: 10 minutes

Yields: 2 to 3

INGREDIENTS:

2 tablespoons unsalted butter

2 tablespoons extra virgin olive oil

1 garlic clove, minced

1 small red onion, diced

2 cups loosely packed Swiss chard, trimmed and chopped

½ cup of dry white wine

½ lemon, juiced, or as needed to taste

¼ cup Parmesan cheese, grated

Salt, to taste (optional)

DIRECTIONS:

1. Place the inner cooking pot in the rice cooker, turn on and press the white rice button to start cooking. Melt in the butter and sauté the garlic and onion for 1 minute, or until soft and fragrant.
2. Stir in the Swiss chard, lemon juice and the wine, season to taste with salt. Close lid and cook for 5 minutes, or until the Swiss chard is almost wilted. Switch to keep warm mode, stir the ingredients and maintain in keep warm mode before serving.
3. Stir in the Parmesan cheese, portion Swiss chard into individual serving bowls, Serve immediately.

ITALIAN PEAS

This delicious rice-and-pea dish is a wonderful way to incorporate both vegetables and starch in one scrumptious side-dish. I love the way the shallots and celery perfectly balance the flavor combination of the chicken stock and white wine – the perfect blend of tastes for a side-dish that's both soothing and irresistible.

Preparation time: 10 minutes

Cooking time: 40 to 45 minutes

Yields: 4

INGREDIENTS:

1 tablespoon of extra virgin olive oil

1 tablespoon ghee

3 shallot, minced

2 stalks of celery, diced

2 to 3 tablespoons of dry white wine

1 cup medium-grain starchy rice, soaked and drained

3 cups low sodium chicken stock

1 cup canned peas, drained

For serving

1 tablespoon butter

3 tablespoons of heavy cream

1⁄4 cup grated Parmesan cheese

DIRECTIONS:

1. Place the inner cooking pot in the rice cooker, turn on and press the white rice button to start cooking. Add the oil and melt the butter. Sauté the shallots and celery until soft, or for 3 to 4 minutes. Pour in the wine and 1 cup of rice, briefly stir and cook for 3 minutes.
2. Add the peas and stock and then close the lid, cook for 30 minutes or until it switches to keep warm mode. Fluff the rice with the serving ladle and cook further if the rice is not yet cooked through.
3. Stir in the cheese, butter and the cream in the inner cooking pot and toss to coat. Close lid and cook for 10 minutes in keep warm mode.
4. Portion into individual serving bowls and serve immediately.

SUCCOTASH

I absolutely love a side of hot and spicy succotash with my dinner, and this recipe below is my go-to favorite. I love that it incorporates healthy okra and tomatoes, along with the classic corn and lima beans, all mixed in with delicious white-wine vinegar, onions and jalapeños. This is a nutritious and delicious side-dish for any meal, so serve it up with a smile – and make sure to get a heaping portion for yourself!

Preparation time: 10 minutes

Cooking time: 25 minutes

Yields: 4

INGREDIENTS:

½ cup diced bacon

1 red onion, diced

1 teaspoon minced garlic cloves

4 ears of corn, kernels cut off

1 large jalapeño, minced

1 cup baby lima beans

2 cups okra, cut into 1-inch pieces

1 cup cherry tomatoes, halved

2 tablespoons of white wine vinegar, or as needed to taste

salt and black pepper, to taste

¼ cup loosely packed fresh basil leaves, chopped

DIRECTIONS:

1. Place the bacon in the inner cooking pot. Place the inner pot in the rice cooker, turn on and press the white rice button to start cooking. Cook the bacon until crisp, remove with a slotted spoon and place on a plate with paper towels.
2. Sauté the onions in the inner cooking pot and cook until soft and translucent. Stir in the garlic and cook for 2 minutes while stirring regularly. Add the beans, okra, corn kernels, jalapeño, tomatoes, wine vinegar, basil, salt and black pepper and stir. Close the lid and cook for 20 minutes or until it switches to keep warm mode.
3. Portion succotash into individual serving dishes and serve warm with bacon bits on top.

STEWED OKRA & TOMATOES

This wonderfully healthy side-dish is a snap to prepare in the rice-cooker, for a wonderful savory vegetable platter that works on the side of any meal. Both okra and tomato are jam-packed with vitamins and nutrients, and the bacon bits and onion in this recipe add a wonderful tangy kick to every bite. This is a great side-dish to serve in the summer months, since it's light enough to enjoy even on the hottest days.

Preparation time: 10 minutes

Cooking time: 20 minutes

Yields: 4

INGREDIENTS:

¼ cup crispy bacon bits

1 medium onion, chopped

1 pound okra, trimmed and cut into 1-inch pieces

1 cup canned diced tomatoes

Salt and coarsely ground black pepper, to taste

DIRECTIONS:

1. Place the inner cooking pot in the rice cooker, turn on and press the white rice button to start cooking.
2. Add the oil and sauté the onions until soft and translucent. Stir in the okra and tomatoes, season to taste with salt and pepper.
3. Close the lid and cook for 15 to 20 minutes. Mix in the bacon bits and stir briefly, close lid and switch to keep warm mode. Maintain in keep warm mode before serving.

MASHED POTATOES

Everyone loves a side of hot mashed potatoes – it's hard to imagine a meal that wouldn't be improved by a helping of creamy spuds. What everyone doesn't know is that they're incredibly easy to prepare in a good rice cooker, with way less muss and fuss than would be required on a stovetop cooker. This recipe incorporates not only butter, but also sour cream and cream cheese to boot, for a dish that's deliciously indulgent and sure to steal the show at your dinner table.

Preparation time: 15 minutes

Cooking time: 2 hours 30 minutes

Yields: 4 to 6

INGREDIENTS:

2 pounds red potatoes, cut into chunks

1 tablespoon minced garlic, or to taste

1 cube chicken bouillon

½ cup sour cream

½ cup cream cheese, softened

½ cup unsalted butter

Salt and ground pepper, to taste

DIRECTIONS:

1. Place the potatoes, garlic, chicken bouillon and salt in the inner cooking pot. Pour water just to cover the potatoes, turn on and press the white rice button to start cooking. Cook for 20 minutes and remove the potatoes with a slotted spoon, transfer the cooking liquid to a separate bowl and set aside.

2. Mash the potatoes with a masher and mix in the cream cheese and sour cream. Add back in enough cooking liquid until desired consistency is achieved.
3. Return the potato mixture into the inner pot, close and cook in keep warm mode for 2 hours. Stir in the butter just before serving.
4. Portion into individual serving bowls, adjust taste and serve warm.

Corn Fritters

If your family loves corn fritters, but you'd rather avoid the unhealthy deep-fried oil that goes with them, you're in luck! This fantastic fritter recipe works perfectly in a well-made rice cooker, crispy and crunchy and scrumptious till the last bite! This is a real crowd-pleasing appetizer or side-dish for any gathering, party, or family meal.

Preparation time: 15 minutes

Cooking time: 20 to 25 minutes

Yields: 3 to 4

INGREDIENTS:

1/2 cup frozen whole-kernel corn, thawed

1/3 cup cooked rice

1 tablespoon all-purpose flour

1/2 teaspoon sugar

1/4 teaspoon baking powder

1/8 teaspoon salt

1/8 teaspoon black pepper

2 large eggs

2 tablespoons margarine or butter

DIRECTIONS:

1. Combine the corn, rice, flour, sugar, baking powder, salt, and black pepper in a mixing bowl and mix until well incorporated. Set aside.
2. In small bowl, whisk the eggs until foamy. Fold the eggs into the mixing bowl with the corn mixture.

3. Place the inner cooking pot in the rice cooker and press the white rice button. Melt the butter. Take about half a cup of the corn mixture and shape it into wide flat fritters, just enough to fit in the inner cooking pot. Close lid and cook for 3 minutes on each side, turn to cook the other side for 3 minutes. Repeat the procedure with the remaining ingredients.
4. Transfer corn fritters to a serving dish and serve warm.

Steamed Corn on the Cob

If you love corn on the cob, but didn't realize how wonderfully easy it is to make perfectly in your rice cooker, prepare to get seriously excited. This lightly seasoned corn cooks up perfectly right in your own kitchen, no barbecue required, for a perfect side-dish to any family meal.

Preparation time: 5 minutes

Cooking time: 20 minutes

Yields: 4

INGREDIENTS:

4 ears corn, husked and halved if needed to fit in the rice cooker

Water, as needed to fill to line 1

2 tablespoons of salt

2 tablespoons butter, for serving

Salt and ground black pepper, for serving

DIRECTIONS:

1. Add water to fill up to line 1 in the inner cooking pot, add salt and place the inner cooking pot in the rice cooker. Turn on and press the white rice button to start cooking. Bring water to a boil.
2. Place the corn on the steam tray and place it in the inner cooking pot, close lid and steam for about 15 minutes. Switch to keep warm mode and cook for 5 minutes more.
3. Remove the steam tray from rice cooker and cover corn with foil, until ready to serve.
4. Brush the corn with butter and season with salt and pepper. Serve immediately.

SOUPS, STEWS AND CHILI

Creamy Potato Soup

Some nights what you really need is hot, creamy, filling comfort food. For those nights (I find they usually come in the dead of winter, during a long work week), this soup is precisely what the doctor ordered. Loaded with beef, vegetables, and gentle savory seasonings, this is a meal that will fill you up in the best possible way.

Preparation time: 15 minutes

Cooking time: 25 minutes

Yields: 6 to 8

INGREDIENTS:

2 cups of ground beef

1 small white onion, diced

1 tablespoon cooking oil

1 large carrot, peeled and diced

1 medium stalk of celery, chopped

2 cups of beef stock

1 cup of water, or as needed

Salt and black pepper, to taste

3 Russet potatoes, peeled and cubed

½ cup of fresh milk

½ cup of cubed Cheddar Cheese

½ cup of canned evaporated milk

2 tablespoons chopped fresh parsley leaves

DIRECTIONS:

1. Place the inner cooking pot in the rice cooker, turn on and press the white rice button to start cooking. Add and heat the oil, add the beef and cook until brown while stirring regularly. Stir in the onions, celery, and carrots and cook until soft and tender. Drain the excess fat, stir in the potatoes and pour in the stock. Add a little water if needed to mostly cover vegetables. Season to taste with salt and pepper, close the lid securely and cook until the potatoes are tender, or until the rice cooker switches to keep warm mode.
2. Stir in the cheese, milk and evaporated milk in the inner cooking pot and briefly stir to combine. Reset the rice cooker, close lid and return to a boil. Cook for about 10 minutes or until the sauce has thickened while stirring regularly.
3. Remove the inner cooking pot and portion soup into individual serving bowls. Serve warm with chopped parsley on top.

CLAM CHOWDER

If you're hankering for a delicious clam chowder but you've never before tried to make one at home, relax and rejoice – this is the recipe for you. This delicious chowder couldn't be easier to prepare in your own kitchen with a rice cooker, and the spice and seasoning mix comes out perfectly every time in the light cream base. This is a wonderful appetizer or full meal to serve at any family gathering or dinner party – and your guests will henceforth think of you as a bona fide clam-chowder expert!

Preparation time: 5 minutes

Cooking time: 35 minutes

Yields: 4 to 6

INGREDIENTS:

2 to 3 tablespoons of unsalted butter

2 medium onions, diced

1 medium stalk of celery, roughly chopped

2 to 3 garlic cloves, minced

2 medium white potatoes, peeled and cubed

2 tablespoons of flour

2 cups of vegetable or chicken stock

1 cup of cream

1 ½ cup of canned clams, drained and chopped

1 bay leaf

½ teaspoon of dried thyme

DIRECTIONS:

1. Place the inner cooking pot in the rice cooker, turn on and press the white rice button to start cooking. Melt the butter and stir in the garlic, onions, celery and bay leaf in the inner pot and sauté until soft and fragrant.
2. Slowly add the flour and cook until lightly brown while stirring constantly. Pour in the stock, and then add the thyme and potatoes. Season to taste with salt and pepper, close lid and cook until the potatoes are tender, or for about 20 minutes.
3. Stir in the clams and cream, cook for about 10 minutes or until the soup has returned to a boil. Remove the inner cooking pot from the rice cooker.
4. Portion the soup into individual serving bowls and serve with your choice of bread.

FRENCH ONION SOUP

French onion soup is a crowd-pleasing yet elegant way to start off any meal or, if you serve large enough portions, a filling meal all on its own! My recipe here uses mozzarella instead of provolone cheese – I just find that it gives the flavors in the soup an extra kick – but feel free to substitute as desired. And have a blast serving up this classic and much-adored favorite!

Preparation time: 10 minutes

Cooking time: 2 hours and 10 minutes

Yields: 8

INGREDIENTS:

3 white onions, sliced into rounds

¼ cup of clarified butter or melted butter

¼ cup of flour

1 to 2 tablespoons of Worcestershire sauce

½ tablespoon sugar

½ teaspoon of coarsely ground pepper

4 cups of beef stock

French bread, sliced into 8 1-inch thick slices

¾ to 1 cup of Mozzarella cheese, shredded

¼ cup of Parmesan cheese, grated

DIRECTIONS:

1. Place the inner cooking pot in the rice cooker, turn on and press the white rice button to start cooking. Add the clarified butter and the onions, cook for about 5 minutes or until the onions are soft and translucent. Stir in the flour, sugar, ground pepper and the Worcestershire sauce in the inner pot and cook for 5 minutes

while stirring regularly. Pour in the stock, close the lid securely and cook for about 2 hours or until the rice cooker switches to keep warm mode.

2. When the onions are very tender, prepare the bread for serving. Top each slice with Mozzarella and Parmesan cheese and set aside.
3. Portion onion soup into individual serving bowls and serve warm with a slice of bread on top.

Butternut Squash Soup

Butternut squash soup is a favorite for my family during Autumn. It is a much-requested starter dish on our Thanksgiving menu. This recipe packs a light kick with some curry and cayenne powder, which perfectly complements the potato and squash in the mix.

Preparation time: 45 minutes

Cooking time: 2 to 3 hours

Yields: 4 to 6

INGREDIENTS:

1 pound of butternut squash, seeded and peeled, diced

1 large potato, peeled and diced

1 red onion, diced

½ tablespoon of curry powder

½ teaspoon of cayenne pepper

Salt and coarsely ground black pepper, to taste

2 to 3 cups of vegetable stock

1 cup of heavy cream

DIRECTIONS:

1. In the inner cooking pot, add the stock, butternut squash, curry powder and the onions. Place the inner cooking pot in the rice cooker, turn on and press the white rice button. Close lid and cook until the squash is tender, or for about 2 to 3 hours. Remove the inner cooking pot from the rice cooker, let it rest to cool.

2. Transfer the mixture into a food processor or blender and pulse until smooth and thick. Stir in the cream and cayenne pepper and briefly pulse to combine.
3. Before serving, reheat the soup in the rice cooker for about 5 minutes. Season to taste salt and pepper and portion soup into individual serving bowls. Serve immediately.

Beef Stew

This recipe is a wintertime staple in my house, and no matter how many times I make it, no one ever seems to get enough of it. How do I know? No leftovers, ever! This savory, hearty classic combines chunks of beef with a healthy array of legumes and vegetables, for nutritious and delicious goodness in every single chunky bite. This is a great dinner to serve when your friends, family, or guests could use a little extra health-giving warmth.

Preparation time: 10 minutes

Cooking time: 1 hour

Yields: 4

INGREDIENTS:

1 tablespoon of olive oil

1 pound of beef stew meat, cut into cubes

1 cup of tomato sauce

1 large onion, diced

2 medium red bell peppers, diced

1 medium stalk of celery, chopped

1 small carrot, peeled and diced

½ cup of canned peas, drained

1 medium potato, peeled and diced

½ cup of canned white beans, drained

2 garlic cloves, minced

1 cup of water or beef broth, more as needed

DIRECTIONS:

1. Place the inner cooking pot in the rice cooker, turn on and press the white rice button to start cooking. Add the oil and heat until it starts to smoke, add the half of beef and cook until browned on all sides. Remove from the inner pot and brown the remaining meat.
2. Return the browned beef and all of the remaining ingredients into the inner cooking pot. Make sure there is enough liquid to mostly cover the vegetables. Cook for about 1 hour or until the beef is tender and the vegetables are soft. Stir the ingredients occasionally while cooking to avoid browning of contents on the bottom of the pot. Season beef stew to taste with salt and pepper and remove the inner cooking pot from the rice cooker.
3. Portion stew into individual serving bowls and serve warm.

Chinese Chili

This Chinese-style chili packs a serious punch – in the best possible way. I love that it incorporates seriously meaty brisket instead of regular ground beef, and the array of peppers and spices in the mix takes the flavor to a whole new level. This is a real crowd-pleaser that's great to serve at a family gathering, or any dinner where you want to serve a feast of a meal.

Preparation time: 10 minutes

Cooking time: 2 hours

Yields: 6

INGREDIENTS:

1 pound of beef brisket, trimmed and cut into 1-inch cubes

3 tablespoons of light soy sauce

3 tablespoons of hoisin sauce

2 red onions, diced

1 tablespoon of oil

2 medium bell peppers, diced and seeded

1 to 2 jalapeños pepper, chopped

1 red hot chili pepper, chopped

3 garlic cloves, minced

1 tablespoon fresh ginger root, grated

2 to 3 teaspoons of crushed Sichuan pepper

2 to 3 teaspoons of five-spice mix

1 cup of beer

1 cup of canned diced tomatoes

2 to 3 teaspoons of cider vinegar

Chili oil, as needed of extra heat

¼ cup of loosely packed fresh cilantro, minced

DIRECTIONS:

1. Place the inner cooking pot into the rice cooker, turn on and press the white rice button and add the oil. Once the oil is hot, add the beef and cook until brown on all sides. Remove from the inner cooking pot and transfer to a bowl.
2. Pour in the hoisin sauce and light soy sauce in the bowl and toss to coat the beef with sauce.
3. Add the bell peppers, onions, chili, jalapeno, garlic and ginger into the inner cooking pot and cook for about 5 minutes, or until the vegetables are soft and aromatic. Stir in the crushed Sichuan peppers, five-spice mix and tomatoes and then pour in the beer. Add the beef back to the inner pot. Close the lid and cook for about 1 ½ hour or until the beef is tender.
4. Pour in the cider vinegar and add more water if the soup is too thick. Stir in the chili oil and adjust seasoning by adding salt and soy sauce. Once the beef is tender, remove the inner cooking pot from heat.
5. Portion into individual serving bowls and serve warm with chopped cilantro on top.

Miso Soup

This classic Japanese soup is pure soothing bliss. And you don't have to get expensive sushi takeout to enjoy it right at home – this recipe couldn't be simpler, and it cooks up easy as pie with a good rice cooker. This soup is usually served as an appetizer, but the protein-rich tofu means it could also work great as a standalone meal. So serve it up and enjoy this warm, health-giving goodness.

Preparation time: 5 minutes

Cooking time: 15 to 20 minutes

Yields: 4

INGREDIENTS:

4 cups Dashi stock

3 to 4 tablespoons of miso paste

1 to 1 ½ cup of silken tofu, cubed

2 medium spring onions, cut into ½-inch bias cuts

DIRECTIONS:

1. Add the Dashi stock into the inner cooking pot and place in the rice cooker. Turn on the rice cooker, press the white rice button and bring the stock to a boil. Stir in the miso paste and tofu, return to a boil and add the spring onions. Remove inner cooking pot from the rice cooker.
2. Portion miso soup into individual serving bowls. Serve immediately.

CURRY LAKSA

This hearty curried laksa – a variation on noodle stew – is a feast unto itself. Loaded with chicken, prawns and tofu, there's a wonderful dose of lean protein in every bite, and I absolutely love the flavor combination of coconut milk, laksa paste, and just a touch of sugar. This is a terrific meal to serve to family or friends!

Preparation time: 15 minutes

Cooking time: 1 hour

Yields: 4 to 6

INGREDIENTS:

3 to 4 tablespoons of ghee or vegetable oil

2 to 3 tablespoon of laksa paste

4 cups of chicken stock

1 tablespoon raw cane sugar

1 pound of chicken thighs, debones and skinned, cut into bite size pieces

½ pound of fresh prawns (with tails), peeled and deveined

2 cups of fresh or canned coconut milk

1 cup of fried tofu, sliced

2 cups of fresh bean sprouts

1 pound of raw rice noodles

fried Asian shallots, for serving

2 tablespoons fresh mint leaves, for serving

Chili Sambal, for serving

Lime wedges, for serving

DIRECTIONS:

1. Place the inner cooking pot into the rice cooker, turn on and press the white rice button to start cooking. Add the oil, stir in 2 tablespoons of laksa paste and cook for about 2 minutes or until fragrant while stirring regularly. Add the sugar, chicken and stock in the inner pot, and then cook until the chicken is cooked through. Stir in the prawns and cook for 3 minutes or until the prawns are half cooked.
2. Stir in the coconut milk, tofu and bean sprouts, and then bring to a gentle boil. Switch to keep warm mode.
3. While cooking the soup with low heat, place the rice noodles in a large bowl and pour in enough boiling water to just cover. Let it stand for 3 minutes or until the rice noodles have softened. Drain and set aside.
4. Portion noodles into individual serving bowls, top with fried shallots and mint. Add ½ teaspoon of chili sambal on top and pour in the laksa soup. Serve immediately with lime wedges.

Chicken Noodle Soup

We all know and love this soup – and my guess is that there are as many different versions of chicken-noodle soup as there are households that dig in to enjoy it. This recipe is my own personal favorite version, loaded with nutritious vegetables, gentle seasonings with egg noodles, and all that warming chicken goodness you'll love. While I've no doubt that your version is absolutely delicious, I urge you to try my chicken-noodle soup the next time you want a proper comfort-food soup – with a little twist!

Preparation time: 15 minutes

Cooking time: 25 minutes

Yields: 6

INGREDIENTS:

1 tablespoon of ghee or melted butter

1 medium stalk of celery, chopped

1 large carrot, peeled and diced

1 large onion diced

1 potato, peeled and diced

1 teaspoon of dried thyme

½ tablespoon of poultry seasoning

4 cups of chicken stock

½ to 1 cup of egg noodles

2 cups of roasted or boiled chicken, shredded or chopped

Fresh parsley leaves, for serving

DIRECTIONS:

1. Place the inner cooking pot into the rice cooker, turn and press the white rice button. Add the ghee, onions, celery and carrots in the inner pot and cook until soft and fragrant.
2. Add the potatoes, dried thyme, poultry seasoning and stock into the inner pot. Close the lid, bring it to a boil and cook until the potatoes are tender.
3. Stir in the chicken and noodles, close the lid and cook for about 20 minutes, or until the noodles have softened. Switch to keep warm mode before serving.
4. Portion noodles and soup into individual serving bowls. Serve immediately with fresh parsley leaves on top.

Bho Kho

This traditional Vietnamese soup is an excellent addition to any meal – or it works great as the star of its own show. The beef shank cooks up succulent and tender, infused with this special mix of ginger, lemongrass, anise seeds, cilantro, basil, and a healthy dose of fresh carrots. You don't have to be a Vietnamese-food fan to love this soup, so serve with a smile and enjoy!

Preparation time: 20 minutes

Cooking time: 2 to 3 hours on low

Yields: 4 to 6

INGREDIENTS:

1 pound of beef shank, cut into 1-inch cubes

1-inch fresh ginger root, sliced into rounds

1 medium stalk of lemongrass, white part (bruised) and green leaves (tied)separated

1 bay leaf

2 star anise seeds

3 cups of beef stock

2 large carrots, peeled and chopped

½ tablespoon annatto seed oil

Lime wedges, for serving

Diced cilantro or green onions, for serving

Sliced jalapenos, for serving

Fresh Basil, for serving

For the Marinade

1 shallot, minced

2 garlic cloves, minced

1 teaspoon smoked paprika

1-inch lemongrass (white part), minced

2 to 3 teaspoons of fish sauce

1 pinch of red chili powder, or as needed for extra heat

1 pinch of ground cinnamon

1 pinch of ground clove

1 pinch of ground anise

Ground black pepper and sugar, to taste

DIRECTIONS:

1. Combine together all ingredients for the marinade in a large bowl and mix it thoroughly. Add the beef and toss to coat evenly with the marinade. Let it stand for at least 1 hour.
2. Place the inner cooking pot into the rice cooker, turn on and press the white rice button to start cooking. Add the annatto seed oil and heat until it starts to smoke, add the beef and brown on all sides. Stir in the bruised lemongrass, star anise seeds, bay leaf and pour in the stock in the inner pot. Add more stock if needed to just cover the meat, close lid and bring to a boil.
3. Cook until the beef is tender, or until the rice cooker switches to keep warm mode. Reset the rice cooker if the beef is not yet ready if it has switched to keep warm mode. If the beef is almost done, maintain keep warm mode for another hour or more.
4. An hour before serving the soup, add the carrots, ginger and season to taste with black pepper, salt and sugar.

Lentil Soup

This classic lentil dish is the ultimate in soup-format comfort food. I love the delicate yet rich array of spices in this recipe, with the toasted cumin and coriander adding a delicious layer to every bite. This is a wonderful soup to serve in the winter months, or at the end of any long day when your friends, family, or guests could use a little extra warming.

Preparation time: 30 minutes

Cooking time: 45 minutes

Yields: 6

INGREDIENTS:

1 to 2 tablespoons of cooking oil

2 medium onions, diced

1 medium carrot, peeled and diced

1 medium stalk celery, chopped

½ tablespoon of salt, or as needed to taste

2 cups lentils, rinsed and drained

1 cup diced tomatoes

4 cups of chicken stock

1/2 teaspoon freshly ground coriander

1/2 teaspoon freshly ground toasted cumin

1/2 teaspoon freshly ground grains of paradise

DIRECTIONS:

1. Place the inner cooking pot into the rice cooker, turn on and press the white rice button to start cooking. Add and heat the oil until it starts to smoke, sauté the onions, celery, carrots and salt until soft and fragrant. Stir in the lentils, coriander, tomatoes, cumin, grains of paradise and the stock. Close the lid, bring to a boil and cook until the lentils are tender. Switch to keep warm mode and wait for about 10 minutes before removing the inner pot from the cooker.
2. Let it stand to lower temperature and transfer into a food processor or blender, pulse until smooth or a coarse mixture.
3. Portion into individual serving bowls and serve immediately.

MOROCCAN LENTIL STEW WITH DATES

This delectable savory stew, sweetened with dates and seasoned with a wonderful array of spices and herbs, is as nutritious as it is delicious. Lentils are an excellent vegetarian source of protein and iron, though this stew is hearty and flavorful enough that it will satisfy meat-eaters and herbivores alike. Dig in and eat well!

Preparation time: 15 minutes

Cooking time: 2 hours

Yields: 4

INGREDIENTS:

1 to 2 tablespoons of cooking oil

1 white onion, finely diced

1 cup canned chickpeas

4 cups of vegetable stock

2 garlic cloves, minced

1 tablespoon fresh cilantro, chopped

1 teaspoon table salt

2 medium stalk of celery, chopped

2 red tomatoes, diced

½ cup lentils, rinsed

1 teaspoon tomato paste

1 teaspoon lemon juice

1 cinnamon stick

1 pinch sweet paprika

1 pinch turmeric

1/2 teaspoon grated ginger

1 pinch coriander powder

1 pinch nutmeg

1 pinch ground pepper

1 pinch clove powder

½ cup vermicelli, broken into pieces

½ cup of dates, pitted and chopped

¼ cup loosely packed fresh parsley leaves, plus whole leaves for garnish

lemon wedges, for serving

DIRECTIONS:

1. Place the inner cooking pot into the rice cooker and press the white rice button. Add the oil and sauté the onions for 5 minutes or until soft and tender. Stir in the chickpeas and pour in the stock. Close the lid and cook for about 30 minutes.
2. Add the garlic, cilantro, celery, tomatoes, lentils, lemon juice, tomato paste, and ground spices into the pot. Close the lid and cook for 30 minutes.
3. Stir in the vermicelli and dates and cook for about 10 minutes or until the noodles have softened. Stir in extra chopped cilantro and parsley, and then remove the inner pot from the rice cooker.
4. Portion into individual serving bowls and serve immediately with lemon wedges.

MOROCCAN CHICKPEA CHILI

This chickpea-based twist on traditional Western chili is a huge crowd-pleaser. The combination of vegetables, seasonings and spices works perfectly – thanks largely to that wonderful ginger root tying all the flavors together. The chickpeas and tomatoes have such a wonderful texture that you don't even miss the meat.

Preparation time: 20 minutes

Cooking time: 20 minutes

Yields: 4

INGREDIENTS:

½ tablespoon oil

1 medium onion, diced

1 medium stalk celery, chopped

1 small carrot, diced

½ teaspoon minced garlic

1 teaspoon cumin

1 teaspoon smoked paprika

1-inch fresh ginger root, grated

½ teaspoon turmeric powder

1 pinch black pepper

1 pinch salt

1 pinch cinnamon powder

½ teaspoon crushed red pepper flakes

1 cup of water

3 tablespoons unsalted tomato paste

2 cups canned chickpeas, drained

1 cup canned diced tomatoes

¼ cup loosely packed fresh cilantro leaves, chopped

2 to 3 teaspoons of lemon juice

DIRECTIONS:

1. Place the inner cooking pot into the rice cooker, turn on and press the white rice button. Add the oil and heat until it starts to smoke. Sauté the onions, garlic, celery, carrots for 5 minutes or until soft and fragrant while stirring occasionally.
2. Add the ground spices, briefly stir and season with salt and pepper. Stir in the tomato paste, tomatoes, and chickpeas and pour in the water. Close the lid and bring it to a boil. Switch to keep warm mode and cook with low heat until the chickpeas are tender. Stir in the cilantro and lemon juice and remove the inner cooking pot from the rice cooker.
3. Portion into individual serving bowls and serve warm.

MIDDLE EASTERN LAMB STEW

I love a good lamb stew, and this Middle Eastern version is as good as it comes. The spice combination in this dish is simply divine, with cumin, coriander, and a healthy dose of garlic. The spinach and chickpeas become perfectly seasoned and the lamb in the stew cooks up perfectly succulent and tender. If you're still looking for a go-to hearty lamb stew, I can't recommend this recipe highly enough.

Preparation time: 40 minutes

Cooking time: 3 hours and 30 minutes to 4 hours

Yields: 4

INGREDIENTS:

1 pound lamb stew meat, cut into 1-inch cubes

1 tablespoon canola oil

½ tablespoon cumin powder

1 teaspoon coriander powder

1 pinch cayenne pepper

1 pinch of salt

Freshly ground pepper, to taste

1 medium onion, diced

½ cup canned diced tomatoes

½ cup chicken stock

1 garlic clove, minced

½ cup canned chickpeas, rinsed

½ cup loosely packed baby spinach

DIRECTIONS:

1. Combine together the oil, cayenne, cumin, salt and pepper in a bowl and mix until well combined. Set aside.
2. Place the inner cooking pot into the rice cooker, add the meat and turn on the rice cooker. Pour in the spice mixture, toss to coat the meat with the mixture and press the white rice button. Add the onions on top, tomatoes, garlic and pour in the stock. Close the lid and cook until the meat is tender, if the rice cooker switches to keep warm mode and the meat is not yet done, reset and continue cooking.
3. When the lamb is tender, stir in the chickpeas and spinach and cook until the spinach is wilted. Remove the inner pot from the rice cooker.
4. Portion meat and vegetables into individual serving bowls and serve immediately.

TOMATO AND CHICKPEA SOUP

This soup is vegetarian-safe – no meat included – but you don't have to be an herbivore to fall head-over-heels in love with these tangy, layered flavors in every bite of this hearty soup. For meat-eaters and veggie-lovers alike, this soup will be a real treat – so whip up a batch today and serve it up, and make sure to get a large portion for yourself before it's all gone!

Preparation time: 5 minutes

Cooking time: 25 minutes

Yields: 4

INGREDIENTS:

1 tablespoon cooking oil

1 red onion, diced

1 medium stalk celery, diced

½ tablespoon cumin

2 cups vegetable stock

1 cup canned plum tomatoes, diced

1 cup canned chickpeas, drained

½ cup broad beans

½ lemon, juiced and zested

½ cup loosely packed fresh coriander leaves, for serving

DIRECTIONS:

1. Place the inner cooking pot into the rice cooker, turn on and press the white rice button. Add the oil and sauté the onions and celery for 5 minutes or until soft and tender. Stir in the cumin, stir to combine and cook for 1 minute.

2. Stir in the tomatoes, chickpeas, broad beans, black pepper and pour in the stock with the lemon juice. Bring to a boil and cook for about 10 minutes or until the beans and chickpeas are tender.
3. Switch to keep warm mode and add the lemon zest and herbs, remove inner pot form the rice cooker. Stir well.
4. Portion into individual serving bowls and serve immediately.

Chicken Soup with Egg-Lemon Sauce

This chicken soup is made absolutely delectable by the delicate yet rich flavor combination of lemon, onion, bay leaf, and an array of spring vegetables. It's easily prepared in your rice-cooker and the result will be a soup that's both hearty enough for a full meal, and elegant enough to serve at a sophisticated gathering or dinner party.

Preparation time: 15 minutes

Cooking time: 1 hour 20 minutes

Yields: 4 to 6

INGREDIENTS:

½ whole chicken, chopped into pieces

2 cups water

½ teaspoon salt

1 medium leek, cleaned and quartered

1 small carrot, peeled and quartered

1 bay leaf

1 tablespoons extra-virgin olive oil

½ cup diced onions

½ cup short-grain rice, rinsed and drained

2 tablespoons lemon juice

1 large egg

½ teaspoon freshly ground pepper

DIRECTIONS:

1. Place the chicken, salt and water in the inner cooking pot and place the inner pot into the rice cooker. Turn on the rice cooker, press the white rice button and bring to a boil. Close the lid and cook for about 30 minutes or until the chicken is cooked through.
2. Skim the foam from the surface and add the leeks, bay leaf and carrots. Close the lid, cook for another 30 minutes or until the vegetables are tender. Remove the chicken with a slotted spoon and set aside to cool, strain the stock and place into a bowl. Set aside.
3. Remove the bones and skin of the chicken and cut meat into cubes. Discard bones and skin.
4. Return the inner cooking pot into the rice cooker, press the white rice button and add the oil. Once the oil is hot, sauté the onions and cook until soft and translucent. Stir in the chicken and rice, sauté for 1 minute and pour in the strained stock. Close the lid and cook for about 20 minutes or until the rice is cooked through.
5. While cooking the rice, whisk together the eggs, lemon juice and pepper in a mixing bowl. Stir in 1 cup of hot stock while whisking constantly. Pour the egg mixture into the pot, stir to combine and season to taste with salt. Switch to keep warm mode and cook with low heat before serving.
6. Portion the soup into individual serving bowls and serve immediately.

Italian Sausage Soup

This recipe has been passed down in my family for generations from an old Italian aunt, and it is effectively my most valuable family heirloom. The sweet Italian sausage and zucchini in this recipe is perfectly offset by the rich blend of spices and seasonings, and the red wine in the base makes it particularly savory. This is the kind of dish that will impress and delight all your friends, family, and guests, so serve it with pride – and a large appetite!

Preparation time: 15 minutes

Cooking time: 45 minutes

Yields: 4 to 6

INGREDIENTS:

½ pound sweet Italian sausage, casings remove and chopped

1 garlic clove, minced

1 medium onion, diced

1 cup of canned whole tomatoes

½ cup dry red wine

2 cups of beef stock

¼ teaspoon dried basil

¼ teaspoon dried oregano

1 medium zucchini, sliced into rounds

1 green bell pepper, chopped

2 tablespoons of fresh parsley leaves, chopped

½ cup fettuccine pasta

Salt and black pepper, to taste

DIRECTIONS:

1. Add 2 cups of water and ¼ teaspoon of salt in the inner cooking pot and place into the rice cooker. Turn on the rice cooker, press the white rice button and bring to a boil. Add the pasta and cook for about 5 minutes or until al dente. Strain the pasta, place in a bowl and set aside.
2. Place the sausage into the inner cooking pot. Place the inner pot into the rice cooker, turn on and press the white rice button to cook the sausage until brown. Remove the sausage with a slotted spoon, reserve 1 tablespoon of cooking fat and drain the excess fat.
3. Add the reserved cooking fat into the inner pot, add the onions and garlic and cook soft and translucent. Return the sausage and stir in the bell pepper, zucchini, tomatoes, red wine, stock, basil, oregano and parsley. Close lid, season to taste with salt and pepper and cook for about 30 minutes, or until vegetables are soft. Stir in the pasta and cook until it returns to a boil. Switch to keep warm mode, and keep it warm before serving.
4. Portion the soup into individual serving bowls and serve immediately.

Spanish Chickpea and Chorizo Soup

This soup is exactly what it sounds like – and boy, is it delicious. If you like the salty, lightly spiced flavor of chorizo and the flavors garlic, onion, and leafy green vegetables, this soup will be perfect for you. It's hearty enough to serve as a main meal, or it works great as a starter for an elegant dinner party. However you serve it, you can't go wrong with this meaty, bean-and-legume-filled hot soup – so have it!

Preparation time: 15 minutes

Cooking time: 1 hour

Yields: 3 to 4

INGREDIENTS:

1 tablespoon of cooking oil

½ cup diced onions

½ tablespoon minced garlic

½ cup diced Spanish chorizo

2 cups of chicken stock

1 cup of canned chickpeas, drained

1 bay leaf

2 cups chopped escarole

2 teaspoons sherry vinegar

½ teaspoon table salt

½ teaspoon black pepper, coarsely ground

1 pinch of red pepper flakes, crushed

DIRECTIONS:

1. Place the inner cooking pot into the rice cooker and add the oil, and turn it on. Press the white rice button and heat the oil. Once the oil is hot, sauté the onions until soft and stir in the chorizo and garlic. Sauté the ingredients until the chorizo are lightly browned and add in the chickpeas, bay leaf and the stock. Close the lid, cook for about 30 minutes or until the meat and chickpeas are thoroughly cooked.
2. Open the rice cooker and open the lid, remove and discard the bay leaf and add in the escarole and remaining ingredients. Close the lid, cook until the escarole is wilted and the soup has returned to a boil. Switch and maintain to keep warm mode before serving.
3. Portion the soup into individual serving bowls and serve immediately.

CALLOS CON GARBANZOS

The marriage of beef, tripe, and chorizo in this hearty, meaty soup is an indulgent, savory delight. This recipe uses a complex blend of spices and seasonings to perfectly compliment the flavors of the meats, while keeping it all tender and succulent and perfectly cooked. This is a great meal to serve at a dinner party where you're really looking to impress your guests, with a dish that's thoroughly filling and delicious – with just a hint of the exotic!

Preparation time: 20 minutes

Cooking time: 1 to 2 hours

Yields: 3 to 4

INGREDIENTS:

1 cup of honeycomb tripe, boiled ahead

1 cup of cooked beef strips

1 cup of beef stock

2 tablespoons of olive oil

1 teaspoon of annatto powder

½ link of chorizo de Bilbao, sliced into thin rounds

1 teaspoon of minced garlic

1 small onion, diced

½ cup of chopped sun dried tomatoes in oil

1 red chili, chopped

¼ cup loosely packed fresh oregano, chopped

1 small potato, peeled and cubes

1 small carrot, peeled and diced

1 bell pepper, seeded and cut into strips

¼ cup canned peas, drained

¼ cup of canned chickpeas, drained

Salt, sugar and black pepper, to taste

DIRECTIONS:

1. Add the oil in the inner cooking pot and the place the inner pot into the rice cooker. Turn on the rice cooker, press the white rice button and heat the oil. Add the chorizo and cook for about 2 minutes while stirring regularly. Add in the garlic, onions, tomatoes, annatto powder, chili and oregano into the pot and sauté for 2 minutes until fragrant.
2. Add in the beef, tripe, carrots, potatoes, peas, chickpeas and bell peppers into the inner cooking pot and pour in the stock. Season to taste with salt, sugar and black pepper, close the lid and cook for about 1 hour or until the sauce has reduced and the ingredients are tender. If the rice cooker has switched to keep warm mode and the meat and tripe are not yet tender, reset and press the white rice button to continue cooking.
3. Stir the ingredients occasionally while cooking. Switch to keep warm mode and cook for 30 minutes with low heat. Add more stock if the sauce is too thick and adjust seasoning. Maintain keep warm mode before serving.
4. Portion into individual serving bowls and serve immediately with rice or crusty bread.

OXTAIL SOUP

This hearty oxtail soup is kicked up a notch by a sensational seasoning mix and a base that includes a little red wine. Don't worry, the alcohol cooks off – making this soup safe for kids, pregnant women, and all– leaving nothing but a sumptuous flavor blend in every succulent bite. Enjoy!

Preparation time: 15 minutes

Cooking time: 2 to 3 hours

Yields: 4

INGREDIENTS:

1 pound oxtail, chopped

1 teaspoon of Italian seasoning mix

½ tablespoon of olive oil

1 cup of beef stock

3 tablespoons of red wine

1 teaspoon of Worcestershire sauce

2 garlic cloves, chopped

½ teaspoon of dried basil leaves

½ teaspoon of dried oregano leaves

1 bay leaf

½ cup canned tomato sauce

1 white onion, cut into wedges

2 small red potatoes, cut in ½-inch cubes

1 medium carrot, cut into sticks

DIRECTIONS:

1. Season the oxtail with Italian seasoning evenly on all sides. Set aside.
2. Add the oil in the inner cooking pot and place the inner pot into the rice cooker. Turn on the rice cooker, press the white rice button and heat the oil. Add the oxtail and brown on all sides while turning occasionally to evenly cook all sides. Remove from the inner pot and set aside.
3. Add the stock, red wine, onions, garlic and Worcestershire sauce into the pot and cook for 1 minute while scraping the brown bits from the bottom. Stir in the oregano, basil, bay leaf, tomato sauce, in the inner cooking pot and return the oxtail. Stir to combine, close lid and cook for about 1 hour and 30 minutes or until the oxtail is done. Reset the rice cooker if it has switched to keep warm mode and the oxtail is not yet done.
4. Once the oxtail is done, add the onion, carrots, and potatoes and cook for about 15 minutes or until the vegetables are tender. Switch to keep warm mode, and maintain low heat to continue cooking the oxtail until very tender.
5. Transfer soup into a serving bowl and serve immediately.

SEAFOOD CHOWDER

This seafood chowder is so good, I'm often tempted to prepare it multiple nights in a row. It's just that delicious, and there never seems to be any leftovers! Feel free to adjust the ratios of vegetables and herbs in this recipe according to taste; for instance, I always like mine with a little extra parsley. However you prepare it, it's very difficult to mess up this scrumptious hot meal.

Preparation time: 10 minutes

Cooking time: 40 minutes

Yields: 4

INGREDIENTS:

½ pound of cod fillets, sliced into bite size pieces

½ cup diced bell pepper

½ cup diced stalk of celery

½ cup of diced white onions

½ cup of canned tomatoes

½ cup of tomato sauce

1 tablespoon of unsalted butter

1 tablespoon of minced fresh parsley

Salt and black pepper, to taste

1 cup white cooked long-grain rice, rinsed

DIRECTIONS:

1. Add the butter in the inner cooking pot and place the inner pot into the rice cooker. Turn on the rice cooker and press the white rice button to melt the butter. Sauté the onions, celery, and bell pepper until soft and fragrant. Stir in the parsley, tomatoes and tomato sauce and cook for 3 minutes while stirring occasionally.
2. Add the fish into the inner cooking pot, briefly stir to combine and close the lid. Bring to a boil and cook until the sauce has thickened. Switch to keep warm mode and cook with low heat until the fish is thoroughly cooked. Season to taste with salt and pepper.
3. Portion the rice into individual serving bowls, top with fish and pour over the sauce. Serve immediately.

Brazilian Salt Cod Stew

This traditional Brazilian fish stew is a true flavor sensation. The unique combination of salted cod with coconut milk and the light tang of onions and olives makes it a wonderful meal to enjoy at a dinner with friends or at any family gathering. For the adults, this stew goes great with a crisp glass of white wine.

Preparation time: 10 minutes

Cooking time: 55 to 60 minutes

Yields: 4

INGREDIENTS:

½ pound salt cod fillets, soaked overnight and rinsed

½ cup of olive oil

1 cup of coconut milk

1 large white onions, sliced into rounds

1 large potato, peeled

3 hard-boiled eggs, quartered

¼ cup of green olives, quartered

Salt and coarsely ground black pepper, to taste

DIRECTIONS:

1. Place the salt cod pieces into the inner cooking pot and pour with milk to cover. Place the inner cooking pot into the rice cooker, turn on and press the white rice button. Close the lid and bring it to a boil. Switch to keep warm mode and cook until the fish is tender. Remove the fish with a slotted spoon and transfer to a bowl. Set aside.

2. Add the potato into the pot, close the lid and cook for about 20 minutes or until tender. Remove potato and slice into thin rounds, and then pour the milk into a bowl. Set aside.
3. Wash the inner cooking pot and wipe with cloth. Return to the rice cooker and coat the bottom with oil. Press the white rice button and layer the onions on the bottom. Place the potato on top of the onions, break the fish into small pieces and place it over the potatoes. Pour milk back into the pot.
4. Add the olives and then the quartered eggs and top with generous amounts of olive oil. Season to taste with salt and black pepper. Close the lid and bring it to a boil. Switch to keep warm mode and cook for 30 minutes, or until the ingredients are cooked through. Maintain keep warm mode before serving.
5. Transfer into a serving bowl and serve immediately.

PUCHERO

This hearty, savory stew comes in many forms. This particular recipe was passed on to me by a friend from the Yucatan, though I'm not sure if it's the traditional preparation for that region. Either way, it's a serious treat for the taste buds, filled with nutritious legumes, vegetables, pork and chicken. This is a nourishing and warm meal to serve after a long day.

Preparation time: 25 minutes

Cooking time: 1 hour 30 minutes

Yields: 4

INGREDIENTS:

1 smoked ham bone

1 cup cooked chicken meat, cut into bite size pieces

½ cup pork belly

1 cup of beef bone broth

½ cup canned chickpeas, drained

1 medium stalk of celery, chopped

1 carrot, peeled and diced

1 tablespoon apple cider vinegar

1 turnip, diced

1 medium leek, chopped

1 red onion, diced or quartered

1 medium potato, peeled and diced

½ head of medium green cabbage, chopped

1 head of pak choi, chopped

DIRECTIONS:

1. Place meat and bones into the inner cooking pot, together with the chickpeas, celery, carrots, leek, turnip and the onions. Add water to fill 2 inches above the ingredients.
2. Stir in the cider vinegar and close the lid, turn on the rice cooker and press the white rice button. Bring to a boil, skim off the foam that floats to the surface and close the lid. Cook for about 1 hour or until the chickpeas are tender and the bone has released most of its flavor.
3. Stir in the potatoes and cook for 20 minutes, or until the potatoes are tender. Remove the meat and bone with a slotted spoon, place meat into a bowl and discard bone. Strain the broth to separate the vegetables and add vegetables into the bowl with the meat.
4. Return the strained stock into the inner cooking pot and return to a boil. Add the pak choi and cabbage and cook until wilted, season to taste with salt and pepper.
5. Portion soup and leafy vegetables into individual serving bowls and top with the vegetables and meat.

ARGENTINE HOMINY STEW

This wonderful hominy stew recipe is an example of a meal that's irresistibly scrumptious – and pretty darn healthy, to boot! With fresh okra, lean pork, and a cornucopia of savory seasonings, this is an excellent meal to prepare when the family could use a hearty dinner that'll do their bodies good.

Preparation time: 10 minutes

Cooking time: 45 minutes

Yields: 4

INGREDIENTS:

1 cup of cooked long-grain rice

1 ½ cups of water

1 teaspoon of salt

1 cup of sliced fresh cut okra

2 cups of chicken stock

1 cup canned hominy, drained

1 jalapeno pepper, finely chopped

Black pepper, coarsely ground to taste

1 teaspoon of crushed cumin seeds

1 cup of sliced pork tenderloin

1 teaspoon of olive oil

2 tablespoons fresh cilantro leaves, finely chopped

DIRECTIONS:

1. Combine together the crushed cumin, ¼ teaspoon of black pepper and salt in a bowl and add the meat. Toss to coat the meat evenly with the spice mixture.
2. Place the inner cooking pot into the rice cooker, press the white rice button and coat with oil. Once the oil is hot, add the meat and brown for 1 minute on each side or until the meat is no longer pink. Remove from the inner pot and slice into thin strips. Set aside.
3. Add the stock and water into the inner cooking pot, place the inner pot into the rice cooker and turn it on. Press the white rice button, close the lid and bring the stock to a boil. When the stock reaches to a boil, stir in the cooked rice, okra, jalapeno, hominy, salt and pepper. When the stock returns to a boil, switch the rice cooker to keep warm mode. Simmer for 20 minutes or until okra is tender.
4. Portion the soup and vegetables into individual serving bowls and top with thin slices of pork meat.

All-American Chili Recipe

Everyone needs a good chili recipe in their repertoire, and this one is my go-to favorite. Football season in my family just wouldn't be complete without at least a few nights gathered around this awesome chili. Of course, it tastes just as great in winter, spring, and fall, as well – there is no bad time to whip up a batch of this all-American goodness!

Preparation time: 10 minutes

Cooking time: 1 hour, 10 minutes

Yields: 4

INGREDIENTS:

2 links of Turkey Italian sausage, casing removed and chopped

1 cup of diced onions

½ cup of diced bell pepper

2 teaspoons of minced garlic

½ pound of ground sirloin

1 jalapeño pepper, chopped

1 to 2 tablespoons of red chili powder

1 tablespoon of brown sugar

2 teaspoons cumin powder

2 tablespoon of tomato paste

½ teaspoon oregano, dried

½ teaspoon black pepper, coarsely ground

2 pinches salt

1 bay leaf

½ cup red wine

1 cup canned tomatoes, chopped

1 cup canned kidney beans, drained

½ cup of Cheddar cheese, grated

DIRECTIONS:

1. Place the inner cooking pot into the rice cooker, turn on and press the white rice button. Add the oil and sausage, cook for 5 minutes or until browned while stirring occasionally. Stir in the onions, ground beef, bell pepper, garlic and jalapeño into the inner pot and cook for about 5 minutes while stirring occasionally.
2. Stir in the chili powder, sugar, cumin, oregano, black pepper, sugar, salt, bay leaf and tomato paste. Cook for 1 minute and stir in the tomatoes, red wine and beans into the inner pot. Close the lid and bring to a boil. Cook for 30 minutes and switch to keep warm mode. Let it cook for 30 minutes with low heat or until the ingredients are tender and cooked through.
3. Open lid and press the white rice button, remove and discard the bay leaf. Cook for 10 minutes and switch to keep warm mode, remove the inner cooking pot from the rice cooker and stir in the cheese.
4. Portion chili into individual serving bowls and serve warm.

MAIN COURSES

ROASTED PORK

There's nothing quite as satisfying as well-cooked, well-seasoned roast pork. This recipe – plus your rice cooker – put that goal easily within reach. I particularly love the scallions and ginger root in this recipe, which perfectly complement the touch of sugar, soy and hoisin sauce for a flavor combination that's both complex and scrumptious. Enjoy!

Preparation time: 10 minutes

Cooking time: 2 hours to 2 hours 30 minutes

Yields: 8

INGREDIENTS:

2 ½-pound of pork butt

½ cup loosely packed scallions

1-inch fresh ginger root, sliced into rounds

4 garlic cloves, crushed

Salt and coarsely ground black pepper, to taste

1 tablespoon of cooking oil

½ cup of light soy sauce

½ cup packed sugar

½ cup of hoisin sauce

DIRECTIONS:

1. Season the meat with generous amounts of salt and pepper and rub on all sides. Tie with a kitchen twine to retain a round form when cooked.
2. Place the inner cooking pot into the rice cooker, turn on and press the white rice button. Coat the bottom of the pan with oil and add the meat when the oil is hot. Add the garlic and brown the meat on all sides, turning to cook the other side.
3. Add in the ginger, scallions, sugar, soy sauce and hoisin sauce and slowly stir the ingredients to combine. Baste the meat with the sauce occasionally while cooking, and turn to cook the other side. Close the lid, cook until the sauce has thickened and switch to keep warm mode to simmer. If the meat is not yet done, reset the rice cooker and add ¼ cup of stock or red wine to avoid the sauce burning. Check regularly and switch to keep warm mode when the meat is thoroughly cooked.
4. When the twisting action of the fork inserted in the meat is effortless or the meat flakes or shreds easily, the meat is done. Remove the meat from the inner cooking pot, transfer to a plate and cover with foil. Let it stand for 10 minutes before serving.
5. Drizzle the sauce on top of the pork before serving. Serve immediately.

Beef Steak

If you think a gourmet steak dinner requires hours of slaving and searing and marinating, for results that may only be so-so, think again. This steak and asparagus recipe is a breeze to prepare, and – thanks to your rice cooker – the result will be a perfectly seasoned, succulently cooked meal every time.

Preparation time: 5 minutes

Cooking time: 10 to 15 minutes

Yields: 1

INGREDIENTS:

1 piece beef steak (1 cm thick)

Salt and crushed black pepper, to taste

4 asparagus spears, trimmed

1 tablespoon butter

DIRECTIONS:

1. Place the inner cooking pot into the rice cooker, turn on and press the white rice button. Melt the butter in the inner pot and add the asparagus. Season with salt and pepper and sauté for about 4 minutes while turning to cook evenly. Remove from the inner cooking pot, place on a plate and set aside.
2. Season the steak with salt and crushed black pepper on both sides. Place it in the inner cooking pot and briefly sear for about 30 seconds on each side. Close the lid and switch to keep warm mode. Cook for 5 minutes on each side with low heat, turn to cook the other side for another 5 minutes. After cooking in keep warm mode, remove from the inner cooking pot and transfer to a plate.

3. If not serving the meat right away, reheat briefly in the rice cooker with the juices on the plate before serving. Remove from the inner pot, transfer to a serving plate and serve with the asparagus spears.

Honey Glazed Chicken

For those who like a touch of sweet with their savory chicken dinner, this recipe couldn't be more wonderful. The tomato paste offers the perfect base for this delicate flavor blend, perfectly bringing out the honey, ginger, and clove, and offset just right by the tangy soy sauce and onion. This is a meal that's both sophisticated enough for a dinner party, but kid-friendly enough for a regular family dinner.

Preparation time: 5 minutes

Cooking time: 35 minutes

Yields: 2

INGREDIENTS:

2 chicken breast fillets

½ cup of local honey

3 tablespoons of light soy sauce

1 small onion, diced

2 tablespoons of tomato paste

2 teaspoons of cooking oil

1 garlic clove, minced

1 teaspoon ginger powder

½ teaspoon of crushed red pepper flakes

DIRECTIONS:

1. Combine together all ingredients except for the chicken in a bowl. Mix the ingredients thoroughly and add the chicken, toss to coat the meat evenly with the sauce. Add into the inner cooking pot and place the inner pot into the rice cooker. Turn on the rice cooker, close the lid and press the white rice button.
2. Cook the chicken for 30 minutes, or until the rice cooker switches to keep warm mode. Turn the chicken after the 15 minutes of cooking. Reset the rice cooker if the chicken is not yet done and add 1 tablespoon of water. Before serving, maintain in keep warm mode to make the chicken more flavorful and tender.
3. Remove the chicken from the inner pot, transfer to a cutting board and when cooled chop into small pieces. Return into the inner cooking pot and toss to coat the meat evenly with the sauce.
4. Transfer to a serving dish and serve immediately.

Beef Broccoli

This dish is a staple on takeout menus, and it's not hard to see why. With hearty beef and wholesome broccoli, this dish packs a wonderfully complete meal in every bite. It's incredibly easy to make at home – and no doubt healthier than those takeout versions – and very difficult to get wrong, with the powerful flavor combo of soy sauce, oyster sauce, and sesame oil. This is a fantastic dinner for any night of the week, which the whole family will enjoy.

Preparation time: 10 minutes

Cooking time: 1 hour

Yields: 4

INGREDIENTS:

1 cup of beef stock

3 tablespoons of light soy sauce

3 tablespoons of oyster sauce

3 tablespoon of sugar

2 to 3 teaspoons of toasted sesame oil

2 garlic cloves, minced

½ pound of thinly sliced beef tenderloin

1 tablespoon of corn starch

1 large head of broccoli, detached florets

DIRECTIONS:

1. Whisk together the stock, oyster sauce, soy sauce, sugar, garlic and sesame oil in a bowl until well incorporated. Add the slices of beef and toss to coat the beef evenly with the sauce.
2. Transfer the meat into the inner cooking pot and pour in the sauce. Place the inner cooking pot into the rice cooker, turn on and press the white rice button. Cook for 20 minutes while stirring occasionally or until the sauce starts to thicken and the meat is cooked through.
3. Close the lid and switch to keep warm mode. Cook for 10 minutes more with low heat until the desired sauce consistency is achieved.
4. If the sauce is not yet thick, whisk together the 2 tablespoons of water and corn starch in a cup and add to the beef and sauce. Stir and reset the rice cooker. Stir in the broccoli and cook until the sauce has thickened and the broccoli is tender.
5. Transfer to a serving bowl or dish and serve immediately. Wonderful served with rice.

GARLIC SHRIMP

This lightly sweetened, spicy-and-savory shrimp preparation is pure delicious elegance. This is a wonderful dish to serve in the summer months, when lean, light protein like shrimp goes down a treat, and the rich and complex flavor combination of garlic, cilantro, coconut milk and jasmine rice will be at their most irresistible.

Preparation time: 5 minutes

Cooking time: 25 minutes

Yields: 4

INGREDIENTS:

2 to 3 teaspoons of cooking oil

1-inch fresh ginger root, minced

1 cup uncooked jasmine rice

1 teaspoon table salt, divided

1 cup plus 3 tablespoons of canned coconut milk, divided

1/4 cup stock

1/4 cup loosely packed fresh cilantro leaves, chopped

2 pounds of fresh shrimps, peeled and deveined

3 garlic cloves, minced

4 to 5 teaspoons of sugar

2 tablespoons of olive oil

½ tablespoon of chili paste

2 teaspoons zest of lime

1 cup of trimmed fresh snap peas, blanched

DIRECTIONS:

1. Combine together the sugar, ¼ teaspoon salt, chili paste, garlic, olive oil in a large bowl and mix until well incorporated. Add the shrimp and snap peas and toss to coat the shrimp evenly with the sauce.
2. Place the inner cooking pot into the rice cooker, turn on and press the white rice button. Add in half of the shrimp into the inner pot and cook for 2 minutes on each side, or until the shrimp turns opaque. Turn the shrimp to cook the other side, remove from the inner pot and cook the remaining shrimp.
3. When the shrimp are done, return the cooked shrimp into the inner pot and add 3 tablespoons of coconut milk and lime zest. Cook until it reaches to a boil, season to taste with salt and pepper and set aside.
4. Return the inner cooking pot into the rice cooker, press the white rice button and add the oil. Once the oil is hot, sauté ginger for 1 minute and stir in ¼ teaspoon salt and the rice. Stir to combine and then pour in 1 cup of coconut milk and ¼ cup of stock. Close the lid and cook until the rice is fluffy and cooked through. When the rice cooker switches to keep warm mode, add the cilantro and fluff the rice with the serving spatula.
5. Portion the rice into individual serving bowls and serve immediately with garlic shrimp on top.

Sesame Ginger Chicken

I love a good sesame-ginger chicken dish, and this recipe produces my all-time favorite version. The deceptively simple flavor combination not only provides an amazing taste in every bite – it also helps keep the chicken tender and succulent. This is a terrific recipe to prepare for a casual dinner with friends, family gathering, or just any time you want a nutritious but delicious chicken dinner. Enjoy!

Preparation time: 10 minutes

Cooking time: 1 hour 45 minutes to 2 hours

Yields: 4

INGREDIENTS:

2 teaspoons sesame oil

4 chicken thighs, bone-in and skinned

3 to 4 tablespoons light soy sauce

1 ½ to 2 tablespoons of brown sugar

½ fresh orange, juiced

1 ½ tablespoons of hoisin sauce

1-inch fresh ginger root, minced

2 garlic cloves, minced

Mixture of 2 teaspoons corn starch and 1 tablespoon water

½ tablespoons of sesame seeds, toasted

2 medium stems of green onions, chopped

DIRECTIONS:

1. Place the inner cooking pot into the rice cooker, turn on and press the white rice button. Add the oil and brown chicken for 4 minutes on each side.
2. Combine together the light soy sauce, orange juice, sugar, ginger, garlic and hoisin sauce in a bowl and mix until well incorporated. Pour the mixture into the inner cooking pot and close the lid. Cook for 15 minutes, turning chicken after the first 10 minutes to cook evenly on both sides. Switch to keep warm mode and cook for 1 hour or until the sauce has started to thicken. Remove the chicken and transfer to plate.
3. Add the water-cornstarch mixture to the inner pot, press the white rice button and cook until the sauce has thickened while stirring regularly.
4. Pour the sauce over the chicken and serve immediately with chopped green onions and sesame seeds on top.

Sweet and Sour Pork

Ok spareribs fans, this one's for you! If you're hankering for tender-cooked pork spareribs with just the right finger-licking delicious marinade, look no further than this awesome recipe. Turns out, you don't need to be a barbecue genius to pull off perfect spareribs! The rice cooker does all the hard work for you, leaving you with nothing to do but enjoy this amazingly cooked meat.

Preparation time: 10 minutes

Cooking time: 40 to 45 minutes

Yields: 4

INGREDIENTS:

1 pound spare ribs, cut into cubes

Marinade

1-inch fresh ginger root, sliced into juliennes

1 tablespoon white sugar

2 tablespoons brown sugar

2 to 3 teaspoons of oyster sauce

1 tablespoon sake or any rice wine

½ tablespoon light soy sauce

½ tablespoon soy sauce

½ cup of water

2 tablespoons cane vinegar

1 tablespoon tomato paste

1 stem of spring onions, chopped for serving

DIRECTIONS:

1. Place the spare ribs into the inner cooking pot and add water to cover the meat. Turn on the rice cooker and press the white rice button. Close the lid and bring to a boil. Transfer into a bowl and let it stand for 10 minutes. Drain and set aside.
2. Combine together all ingredients for the marinade in a non-reactive container and mix it thoroughly until well incorporated. Pour the marinade into the bowl with meat and toss to coat the meat evenly. Cover and marinate and chill for 1 hour.
3. Turn on the rice cooker and press the white rice button, add the meat and brown on all sides for about 5 minutes. Pour in the remaining marinade, briefly stir and close the lid. Cook for about 30 minutes or until the sauce has thickened. Stir the ingredients after the first 15 minutes to keep the sauce from burning.
4. When the meat is done, switch to keep warm mode and let it cook with low heat before serving. Check the meat for the tenderness you desire.
5. Transfer to a serving dish or bowl and serve immediately with chopped spring onions on top.

Thai Chicken

It can be difficult to achieve that inimitable Thai-style flavor combination at home, but this recipe lays it all out and gets it right every time. The combination of sweet and spicy, infused with tangy ginger root and green onion with an aromatic sesame-oil base, is everything you could possibly want in a Thai-chicken entrée – so forget the expensive takeout, and make it right in your own kitchen! And of course, get ready for rave reviews.

Preparation time: 15 minutes

Cooking time: 30 to 35 minutes

Yields: 3 to 4

INGREDIENTS:

½ cup of light soy sauce

4 garlic cloves, minced

1-inch fresh ginger root, minced

1 tablespoon of hot chili sauce, or as needed for extra heat

1 pound chicken thighs, skin removed

1 medium green onion, chopped

2 to 3 teaspoons of toasted sesame oil

2 teaspoons of brown sugar

1 red onion, sliced into rounds

½ cup of water

2 to 3 tablespoons of peanut butter

DIRECTIONS:

1. Combine together the garlic, ginger, light soy sauce and hot chili sauce in a bowl and mix it thoroughly until well combined. Add the chicken and toss to coat the meat evenly with the sauce. Cover bowl and marinate for at least 1 hour.
2. Place the inner cooking pot into the rice cooker, turn on and press the white rice button. Add the sesame oil and sauté the onions until soft, stir in the chicken and marinade and cook for 5 minutes while stirring occasionally.
3. Add ½ cup of boiling water, close lid and cook for 20 minutes, or until the chicken is tender and cooked through. Switch to keep warm mode and simmer for 10 more minutes. Stir in the peanut butter and sugar, mix well and transfer to a serving platter. Pour the sauce on top and serve immediately with chopped green onions on top.

Singapore Chili Prawns

These awesome Singapore-style prawns are the perfect mix of sweet and spicy – just the thing to satisfy a palate looking for a classic Asian flavor combination in every bite of this lean-protein seafood dish. This recipe is a wonderful choice for a party or regular family dinner alike, both nutritious and delicious, so serve it up and eat happy!

Preparation time: 15 minutes

Cooking time: 20 minutes

Yields: 4

INGREDIENTS:

Sauce:

¾ cup of water

¼ cup of ketchup

2 to 3 tablespoons of brown sugar, as needed to taste

1 tablespoon of corn flour

½ tablespoon dark miso

1 pinch of salt

Prawns:

2 cups of fresh prawns, rinsed and drained, sliced across the back and deveined

2 tablespoons of cooking oil

6 garlic cloves, minced

6 red chilies, chopped

1 medium whole egg

1 large scallions, cut into long 2-inch pieces

½ lime, juiced

¼ cup loosely packed fresh cilantro leaves, cut into chiffonades

DIRECTIONS:

1. Combine together all ingredients for the sauce in a bowl and mix it until well combined. Set aside.
2. Place the inner cooking pot into the rice cooker, turn on and press the white rice button. Add the oil and sauté the garlic and chilies for 2 minutes or until lightly brown and aromatic. Add the prawns and cook for 3 minutes, or until opaque while turning to cook the other side. Pour in the sauce mixture and briefly stir to coat the shrimp.
3. Break the egg and slowly add into the inner pot, streak the egg with a fork to form long white streaks in the sauce. Close the lid and switch to keep warm mode. Cook for 10 minutes and stir in the lime juice and scallions. Close the lid and maintain in keep warm mode before serving.
4. Transfer the prawns to a serving platter, pour the sauce on top and serve immediately.

Kung Pao Shrimp

This classic shrimp dish is one of those meals that – as much as you'd like them – you'll never have any leftovers, because it's that delicious. This is a simple and straightforward recipe that delivers the traditional flavors of the dish, with the only update being the ease of preparation in the rice cooker. I love this shrimp, and I know you will too – just make sure to get a portion for yourself before it's all gone!

Preparation time: 20 minutes

Cooking time: 20 to 25 minutes

Yields: 4

INGREDIENTS:

For the Shrimp

1 tablespoon of sake

1 tablespoon of cornstarch

½ teaspoon of salt

1 pound fresh shrimp, peeled and deveined

For the Sauce

2 teaspoons of sugar

3 tablespoons of water

2 to 3 teaspoons of balsamic vinegar

2 to 3 teaspoons of light soy sauce

½ tablespoon cornstarch

½ tablespoon of toasted sesame oil

Remaining Ingredients

1 tablespoon canola oil

½ cup green bell pepper, sliced into strips

2 teaspoons minced garlic

1-inch fresh ginger root, minced

3 dried hot red chili, crushed

2 tablespoons dry-roasted peanuts, chopped

2 cups of cooked rice

DIRECTIONS:

1. Combine together the sake, cornstarch and salt in a bowl until well combined. Add the shrimp and toss to coat evenly with the cornstarch mixture. Set aside.
2. In a separate bowl, combine together all ingredients for the sauce until well combined. Set aside.
3. Place the inner cooking pot into the rice cooker, turn on and press the white rice button. Add the oil and sauté the garlic, ginger, bell pepper and chilies until lightly brown and aromatic. Stir in the shrimp mixture and cook for 5 minutes or until the shrimp turns opaque. Add the sauce, briefly stir and close the lid. Cook for 5 minutes or until the sauce has thickened. Switch to keep warm mode and cook for 15 minutes more, or until the sauce has thickened.
4. Portion rice into individual serving bowls or dishes. Add shrimp and sauce and serve immediately with chopped peanuts on top.

Saudi Fish Curry

This spicy, tangy fish curry is the ideal entrée to serve when you want a filling meal without a ton of red meat. This recipe came to me from a friend of Saudi Arabian descent, and my family can't get enough of it. I particularly love the way the ginger root infuses the flavor of every bite, and of course, how simple it is to prepare in the rice cooker.

Preparation time: 15 minutes

Cooking time: 40 minutes

Yields: 4 to 6

INGREDIENTS:

1 pound white fish fillets, patted dried and cut into serving portions

table salt, to taste

2 tablespoons of clarified butter/ghee (butter or oil)

1 large onion, diced

1-inch piece of fresh ginger root, minced

1 teaspoon minced garlic

½ tablespoon chili powder

½ tablespoon Baharat spice mix (Baharat is a Middle Eastern all- purpose seasoning)

½ tablespoon ground turmeric

1-inch piece of cinnamon bark

1 cup of canned diced tomatoes

1 loomi (dried lime), punctured with holes

½ cup of water

DIRECTIONS:

1. Season fish with salt and set aside.
2. Place the inner cooking pot into the rice cooker, turn on and press the white rice button. Add the ghee and sauté the onions, ginger, garlic, chili powder, Baharat spice, turmeric and cinnamon bark and cook until lightly brown and aromatic. Stir in the loomi, tomatoes and water in the pot and season with salt. Close the lid and bring to a boil. Switch to keep warm mode and simmer for 15 minutes.
3. Stir in the fish, close the lid immediately and cook for 20 minutes, or until the fish is thoroughly cooked.
4. Remove the cinnamon and loomi and discard. Remove the fish with a slotted spoon and pour the sauce on top of the fish. Serve immediately.

Chicken Tikka Masala

This classic Indian chicken dish is a favorite around the world, and with good reason. The combination of sweet-and-spicy flavors in the spice and marinade mixture is truly a taste sensation, and our friends, family, and guests will all be impressed that you made this chicken right in your own kitchen, without resorting to takeaway – so get ready to be showered with compliments as you enjoy this delicious meal!

Preparation time: 10 minutes, plus 2-4 hours for marinating

Cooking time: 45 minutes

Yields: 4 to 6

INGREDIENTS:

For the spice mixture

3 tablespoons smoked paprika

3 tablespoons ground cumin

1 ½ tablespoons ground coriander

1 ½ tablespoons ground turmeric

½ tablespoon cayenne pepper

For the marinade

1 ½ pounds chicken thighs, skinned and cut into small pieces

¾ cup of plain yogurt

1 teaspoon minced garlic

1-inch piece fresh ginger root, minced

1 lemon, juiced

Other ingredients

2 1/2 tablespoons butter, divided

1 red onion, diced

1 tablespoon minced garlic

1 cup of canned diced tomatoes

¾ cup of cream

½ cup loosely packed fresh cilantro leaves, roughly chopped

Oil or butter, for greasing

DIRECTIONS:

1. Combine all ingredients for the spice mix in a bowl and mix until well combined. Reserve half of the mixture while using the other half with the chicken.
2. Mix half of the spice blend with the other marinade ingredients and marinate chicken for 2 to 4 hours.
3. Place the inner cooking pot into the rice cooker, turn on and press the white rice button. Add and melt 2 tablespoons of butter and brown the chicken on all sides until the chicken is thoroughly cooked. Remove from the inner cooking pot and set aside.
4. Add ½ tablespoon of butter into the inner cooking pot, sauté the onions and garlic until lightly brown and soft. Stir in the reserved spice mix and tomatoes, close the lid and cook for 15 minutes. Remove the mixture from the inner cooking pot, transfer to a bowl and let it cool. Transfer to a food processor and puree until smooth.
5. Return the pureed mixture into the inner cooking pot with the chicken, close the lid and bring to a boil. Switch to keep warm

mode and cook for 20 minutes, or until the chicken is done. You can maintain in keep warm mode for 4 hours.

6. Before serving, stir in the cream and cilantro, reset the rice cooker and bring to a boil.

7. Transfer the chicken and sauce to a serving dish and serve immediately.

CHICKEN TANGINE

If you haven't tried the lightly spiced, saffron-seasoned goodness that is chicken tangine, this recipe offers the perfect opening. This traditional eastern dish is awesome to serve at a family gathering or elegant dinner party alike, and the meat and marinade both are incredibly simple to prepare in the rice-cooker. This dish will add a taste of the exotic to any meal, so get on it and enjoy!

Preparation time: 15 minutes

Cooking time:45 minutes

Yields: 4

INGREDIENTS:

1 teaspoon of extra virgin olive oil

1 pound of chicken, trimmed and cut into cubes

3 threads of saffron

1 red onion, diced

1 cup white long-grain rice, rinsed

2 cups chicken stock

1 ½ cup beef stock

1 cup green olives, stuffed with semi-dried tomatoes

DIRECTIONS:

1. Place the inner cooking pot into the rice cooker, turn on and press the white rice button to start cooking. Add the oil and brown half of the chicken on all sides. Remove and brown the remaining chicken. Transfer to a plate and set aside.

2. Add the saffron and onions and cook until soft and aromatic. Stir in the rice and add the stock, close lid and bring to a boil. Cook for about 5 minutes.

3. Add the chicken on top, close the lid and cook for 30 minutes or until the rice cooker switches to keep warm mode. When the chicken and rice are thoroughly cooked, remove the chicken and place on a plate. Add the olives into the rice and fluff with the serving spatula.

4. Portion the rice onto individual serving plates and serve with chicken on top.

BRAISED LAMB CHOPS

Well-braised lamb chops are one of the great gastronomic pleasures – but they can be difficult to get right, and who wants to have to go to a restaurant every time they want this succulent, savory delight? This recipe gets those chops perfectly cooked every time, ideally seasoned, and with a good rice-cooker it's basically foolproof. So go on and indulge – these chops will be the star of your dinner table, and rightly so!

Preparation time: 20 minutes

Cooking time: 3 hours

Yields: 4

INGREDIENTS:

1 ½ tablespoons of extra virgin olive oil
4 lamb chops, chopped in to 2 portions
1 white onion, diced
½ cup of chicken stock
½ cup of white wine
¼ cup of sun dried tomatoes
½ tablespoon of dried thyme
¼ teaspoon of cumin powder
1 cup canned white beans, drained
Salt and crushed black pepper, to taste
2 cups of cooked rice, for serving

DIRECTIONS:

1. Place the inner cooking pot into the rice cooker, turn on and press the white rice button to start cooking. Use olive oil to brown the lamb chops on both sides or for about 20 minutes. Remove lamb chops and set on a plate.
2. Add the onions into the inner cooking pot and cook until soft. Stir in the thyme, tomatoes, cumin, white wine and the stock.

Add lamb chops back to the inner pot. Close the lid securely and bring to a boil. Cook for about an hour and switch to keep warm mode. Cook for 1 more hour with low heat or until the lamb is cooked through.

3. Stir in the beans and reset the rice cooker, cook for 30 minutes or until the lamb is very tender and the beans are cooked through. Season to taste with salt and pepper.

4. Portion the rice into individual serving bowls and serve warm with lamb and sauce on top.

MEDITERRANEAN CHICKEN RICE

A light and savory chicken dish that's filling enough for cold months, but refreshing enough to be perfectly suitable in the warm months, this Mediterranean chicken and rice dish is an excellent go-to dish for dinner parties, family gatherings, or any supper that you really want to hit the spot. I love the addition of lemon zest to the seasoning combination in this recipe, which really helps give the chicken a kick. This is one of my all-around favorite chicken dishes, and I trust it'll soon become one of yours, too!

Preparation time: 5 minutes

Cooking time: 20 minutes

Yields: 4 to 6

INGREDIENTS:

1 ½ tablespoons of cooking oil

1 white onion, diced

1 crushed garlic clove

1 cup cooked, shredded chicken meat

2 cups of short-grain rice, rinsed

2 teaspoons poultry seasoning

2 tablespoons of lemon zest

¼ cup of loosely packed fresh parsley leaves, minced

Crushed black pepper, to taste

boiling water

DIRECTIONS:

1. Place the inner cooking pot into the rice cooker, turn on and press the white rice button. Add the oil and sauté the onion and garlic until soft and translucent. Stir in the rice and chicken and sauté for 2 minutes. Pour in with boiling water to fill up to line 2. Add the poultry seasoning and stir to combine, close the lid and cook until the rice is tender or until it switches to keep warm mode. Season with crushed pepper, stir and cook for 5 more minutes.
2. Pour the contents from the inner cooking pot into a strainer to separate the rice and chicken from any remaining water. Return the rice and chicken into the inner cooking pot, add the lemon zest and parsley and toss to combine.
3. Portion into individual serving dishes and serve immediately.

ITALIAN MEATBALLS

This recipe packs the entirety of an Italian linguini-and-meatball feast into a single easy-to-prepare dish, and it gets those classic flavors just right. This is the perfect meal to prepare for the family after a long day, when you don't have much time but when everyone's bringing a big appetite. The linguini and meatballs won't let them down – and it couldn't be simpler to put together!

Preparation time: 10 minutes

Cooking time: 30 to 40 minutes

Yields: 4 to 6

INGREDIENTS:

1 cup of ready-made marinara sauce

3 cups of water

½ pound of linguini pasta

1 pound of frozen meatballs

2 teaspoons of minced garlic

¼ cup of loosely packed fresh parsley leaves, minced

1 teaspoon of Italian mixed herbs

¼ cup Parmesan cheese, grated

DIRECTIONS:

1. Place the inner cooking pot into the rice cooker and add all ingredients except for the pasta, meatballs and Parmesan. Turn on the rice cooker and press the white rice button. Stir to combine the ingredients, close the lid and bring to a boil.

2. Add the pasta and meatballs and cook for about 20 minutes or until the pasta is cooked to al dente and the meatballs are cooked through.
3. If the sauce is not thick and the pasta is not yet done, reset the rice cooker and cook until the desired thickness is achieved or until the pasta is done.
4. Portion into individual serving dishes and serve immediately with grated Parmesan cheese on top.

SPICY LEMON SPANISH CHICKEN

The rich and zesty flavor combination in this amazing chicken dish makes it the perfect entrée to serve when you are looking to show your family some love. The paprika and garlic perfectly season the chicken, and all the veggies in the dish help keep everything juicy, tender and healthy.

Preparation time: 20 minutes

Cooking time: 3 hours

Yields: 4

INGREDIENTS:

2 tablespoons of flour

1 ½ tablespoons of smoked paprika

2 to 3 teaspoons of garlic powder

Salt and coarsely ground pepper, to taste

4 to 6 chicken thighs

3 to 4 tablespoons of canola oil

1 cup of canned stewed tomatoes

1 large bell pepper, seeded and diced

1 white onion, sliced into rounds

3 tablespoons of tomato paste

2 cups of low sodium chicken stock

1 cup of long-grain rice, rinsed and drained

1 teaspoon of dried crushed red pepper

1 lemon, juiced and zested

½ cup pimiento stuffed green olives

DIRECTIONS:

1. Combine together the flour, salt, pepper, garlic powder, paprika in a bowl and add the meat. Toss to coat the chicken.
2. Place the inner cooking pot into the rice cooker, turn on and press the white rice button to start cooking. Add and heat the oil until smoking, add the chicken and brown for about 5 minutes on each side. Turn to brown the other side and transfer onto a plate.
3. Add the tomatoes, onions and bell peppers into the inner cooking pot. Return the chicken into the pot and place it over the vegetables, pour in the tomato paste and the stock and close the lid. Cook for 1 hour or until the chicken is cooked through, briefly stir and switch to keep warm mode. Simmer for another 1 hour or until the sauce has reduced and thickened.
4. Remove the chicken mixture, transfer to a large bowl and cover to keep it warm. Add the rice, crushed red pepper, lemon juice and zest of lemon. Pour in water to fill up to line 2 and season to taste with salt and pepper. Press the white rice button and cook until the rice is tender and cooked through, or until it switches to keep warm mode. Fluff the rice with the serving spatula and portion into individual serving dishes.
5. Top each dish with chicken and vegetables, drizzle with extra lemon juice on top and serve immediately.

Beef Burgundy

This aromatic and savory dish is a traditional specialty in rural France. But you don't have to travel to the actual Burgundy region to enjoy it, nor even fork out the cash at a fancy French restaurant. With your rice-cooker, the beef and sauce will come out perfectly tender and filled with flavor. Who says haute cuisine has to be difficult? Not me, that's for sure!

Preparation time: 15 minutes

Cooking time: 2 hours

Yields: 4 to 6

INGREDIENTS:

1 pound beef chuck roast, cut into 1-inch cubes

2 large carrots, peeled and diced

2 cups of canned mushrooms, quartered or halved

½ cup of onion wedges

1 teaspoon of minced garlic

1 bay leaf

½ teaspoon salt and ½ teaspoon of black pepper, to taste

½ to 1 teaspoon of dried thyme leaves

¾ to 1 cup of beef stock

¾ cup red wine

3 tablespoons of tomato paste

1 ½ tablespoons of flour

3 to 4 tablespoons of water

2 cups cooked egg noodles

DIRECTIONS:

1. Place the beef, carrots, onions, mushrooms, bay leaf, garlic, thyme, black pepper, salt, stock, wine and the tomato paste into the inner cooking pot. Place the inner cooking pot into the rice cooker, turn on and press the white rice button. Close the lid and cook for about 1 hour and 30 minutes, or until the beef is almost tender.
2. While cooking the beef, combine together the flour and water in a bowl and mix until the flour is completely dissolved. After one and a half hours, pour the mixture into the inner cooking pot and briefly stir to combine. Switch to keep warm mode and cook until thick and the beef is thoroughly cooked.
3. Portion the cooked noodles into individual serving dish or bowls and serve immediately with beef stew on top.

RATATOUILLE

This warming and wonderful dish is the perfect vegetable-filled meal to serve on a chilly day in autumn or winter, filled with nutrients and rich flavors that will fill everyone up and leave a smile on their faces. It's incredibly easy to prepare with a rice-cooker, so go ahead and make it a regular on your meal roster because everyone will love it.

Preparation time: 20 minutes

Cooking time: 1 hour 15 minutes

Yields: 4

INGREDIENTS:

1 cup of diced carrots

1 cup diced potatoes

1 cup chopped zucchini

1/2 white onion, diced

2 red tomatoes, seeded and diced

1 teaspoon minced garlic

1 ½ tablespoons of cooking oil

½ tablespoon of dried basil

Crushed black pepper, to taste

Table salt, to taste

1 cup of vegetable stock

1 tablespoon minced fresh rosemary leaves

1 tablespoon minced fresh thyme leaves

DIRECTIONS:

1. Place the inner cooking pot into the rice cooker, turn on and press the white rice button. Add the oil and sauté the onions, garlic and tomatoes until soft and tender. Stir in the diced vegetables, dried herbs and season to taste with salt and pepper. Stir to combine and pour in the stock. Close the lid and cook for 1 hour or until the vegetables are tender and cooked through.
2. Switch to keep warm mode, briefly stir and cook for another 5 minutes. Transfer to a serving dish and serve immediately.

SHRIMP JAMBALAYA

This jambalaya recipe has been in my family for generations, but somehow it never gets old. The spices and seasonings in this preparation perfectly highlight the juicy textures in both the shrimp and the sausage, and the healthy helpings of veggies in every serving ensure that this really is a complete meal all on its own. This is a perfect dinner to prepare when you want to make a real family feast, without spending hours in the kitchen.

Preparation time: 15 minutes

Cooking time: 30 minutes

Yields: 4 to 6

INGREDIENTS:

1 cup canned button mushroom, halved

2 garlic clove, finely minced

1 link of sweet Italian sausage, casing removed and chopped

1 small red onion, finely diced

1 small bell pepper, diced

2 ½ cups of chicken stock

2 cups of cooked shrimp, peeled and deveined

1 tablespoon of clarified butter

1 ½ cups of long-grain white rice

1 cup canned diced tomatoes

1 teaspoon of cayenne pepper

DIRECTIONS:

1. Place the inner cooking pot into the rice cooker, turn on and press the white rice button. Add the sausage and cook until brown while stirring occasionally. Drain the excess fat and add the clarified butter, stir in the garlic, onions, bell pepper and mushrooms and cook for 5 minutes, until the onions are soft and the vegetables are tender.
2. Stir in the remaining ingredients, briefly stir to combine and close the lid. Bring it to a boil and cook for about 15 to 20 minutes, or until the rice is cooked through. When the rice is done and the rice cooker has switched to keep warm mode, fluff the rice with the serving spatula.
3. Maintain in keep warm mode for 10 minutes and portion into individual serving bowls. Serve warm with extra cayenne pepper for added heat.

CHICKEN AND BARLEY STEW

If you're not used to cooking with barley, fear not. The hull-free (or "pearled") barley in this recipe behaves much like rice, meaning it's ideal for easy preparation in the rice cooker, along with being a seriously nutritious whole cereal grain. The woody flavor and lightly chewy texture of barley also makes it a wonderful addition to this wholesome chicken stew. Its taste and consistency working perfectly with the succulent meat and fresh cooked veggies. This is one of those heaven-sent dishes that you can prepare entirely in the rice-cooker, no muss and no fuss, and the result is a hands-down delicious meal every time.

Preparation time: 5 minutes

Cooking time: 30-40 minutes

Yields: 4

INGREDIENTS:

2 boneless, skinless white-meat chicken breasts, cut into large bite-sized chunks

3 large carrots, rinsed, peeled and diced

2 medium-sized stalks of celery, rinsed and diced

1 large white onion, peeled and chopped

3 cups of chicken broth

1 cup of uncooked pearled barley

8 ounces of canned tomatoes, undrained, diced into chunks

1 teaspoon of dried ground thyme

2 tablespoons of fresh parsley, rinsed and patted dry, finely minced

DIRECTIONS:

1. Fill the inner cooking pot with the chicken broth, then add the chicken, carrots, celery, onion, barley, canned tomatoes and juice, parsley, and thyme. Use a wooden spoon to stir all ingredients thoroughly until evenly mixed, then close the lid, turn on the rice cooker, and press the white rice button.
2. Cook for 30 minutes, or until the chicken is fully cooked through and all the vegetables have softened and are releasing fragrance. The liquid in the chicken broth and tomato juice will have largely been absorbed by the barley, leaving a thick stew consistency.
3. Either portion the stew into individual serving bowls and serve directly, or switch the rice cooker to keep warm mode for up to two hours before serving.

CLASSIC BEEF STEW

This hearty American classic marries traditional flavors with tons of fresh vegetables for a dish that's as warming and filling as can be, while also being pretty darn healthy to boot. My family and I like our beef stew chunky in every bite, so I avoid dicing the meat or veggies any smaller than 1-inch cubes, though feel free to cut them smaller if desired – it won't affect the cooking times. A good rice-cooker will ensure that this stew comes out excellent every time.

Preparation time: 15 minutes

Cooking time: 2 hours

Yields: 4 to 6

INGREDIENTS:

½ cup of all-purpose flour, sifted to remove lumps

½ teaspoon of salt

½ teaspoon of ground black pepper

1 pound beef chuck roast, cut into 1-inch cubes

1 tablespoon of olive oil

1 ½ cups water

1 large white onion, peeled and diced

1 ½ tablespoons of Worcestershire sauce

½ tablespoon of lemon juice

1 large clove of garlic, peeled and minced

½ teaspoon of white sugar

½ teaspoon of paprika

2 medium-sized potatoes, washed, peeled and diced

3 large carrots, washed, peeled and sliced

3 large stalks of celery, washed and diced

1/8 teaspoon of ground allspice

2 cups of cooked white rice

DIRECTIONS:

1. Place the beef, celery, carrots, potatoes, onion, garlic, salt, pepper, Worcestershire sauce, lemon juice, sugar, paprika, allspice, and olive oil into the inner cooking pot, stirring all ingredients with a wooden spoon to combine evenly.
2. Place the inner cooking pot into the rice cooker, turn on and press the white rice button. Close the lid and cook for about 1 hour and 30 minutes, or until the beef is almost tender.
3. While it's cooking, combine together the flour and water in a separate bowl and mix until the flour is completely dissolved. After one and a half hours, pour the water-and-flour mixture into the inner cooking pot and briefly stir with the wooden spoon to combine.
4. Switch to keep warm mode and cook until the sauce is thick and the beef is thoroughly cooked.
5. Portion the cooked brown rice into individual serving dishes or bowls, top with equal portions of the beef stew, and serve immediately while hot.

TOMATO AND TILAPIA HOTPOT

I'm sure you already knew that a diet rich in vegetables was good for the heart. Apparently succulent tilapia and savory cooked tomatoes are great for your heart. Even better, this fish and vegetable hotpot makes for an absolutely sumptuous meal – whether or not one is concerned about their heart. Who knew looking out for cardiovascular health could taste so delicious?

Preparation time: 10 minutes

Cooking time: 15-20 minutes

Yields: 4

INGREDIENTS:

½ pound of tilapia fillets, sliced into bite size pieces

1 tablespoon of corn or canola oil

1 large green bell pepper, seeded and diced

1 large carrot, rinsed, peeled and sliced

1 medium-sized white onion, peeled and diced

1 pound of canned tomatoes, with no salt added, diced, in their own juice (undrained)

1 cup water

1 medium-sized baking potato, rinsed and peeled, diced

1 teaspoon of salt-free Cajun seasoning-blend

½ teaspoon of salt

1 cup cooked wild rice, rinsed

DIRECTIONS:

1. Add the oil in the inner cooking pot and place the inner pot into the rice cooker. Turn on the rice cooker and press the white rice button to heat the oil. Keep the lid open for now.
2. Add the carrot, potato, onion, and bell pepper to the inner cooking pot, stir with a large wooden spoon, then close the lid and allow to sauté for 3 minutes, after which the vegetables should have softened and become fragrant.
3. After 3 minutes, add the diced tomatoes, tomato juice, water, salt, and Cajun seasoning to the inner cooking pot. Stir again with the wooden spoon, then close lid and cook for another 3 minutes.
4. After 3 minutes, add the tilapia into the inner cooking pot, gently stir with the wooden spoon, and close the lid. Bring to a boil, then switch to keep warm mode and cook with low heat until the tilapia is thoroughly cooked, approximately another 5 minutes.
5. Portion the cooked wild rice into individual serving bowls, then spoon the tilapia, tomatoes, broth and vegetables on top. Serve immediately while hot.

Louisiana Gumbo

One dinner that is sure to get my whole family around the dinner table with huge smiles is New Orleans gumbo. There are many variations of this seafood-and-sausage goodness, simmered in a savory beef-and-tomato broth. My preferred version, presented here, uses succulent shrimp and juicy pork-and-beef sausage, dried ground sassafras, okra, and just a touch of hot sauce. From my happy-smiley dinner table to yours, eat up and have fun!

Preparation time: 15 minutes

Cooking time: 25 minutes

Yields: 4

INGREDIENTS:

2 links of pork-and-beef sausage, casings removed, crumbled

2 cups of cooked shrimp, peeled and deveined

2 cups of beef broth

2 large stalks of celery, rinsed and chopped

1 large white onion, peeled and diced

1 large green bell pepper, rinsed and seeded, diced

½ cup of fresh okra, sliced and scooped with the pods removed

1 teaspoon of hot sauce or chili sauce (chef's choice – I usually use either Tabasco or Sriracha)

1 cup of canned tomatoes, drained and diced

1 teaspoon of dried ground sassafras (often sold as "filé powder")

½ teaspoon of Old Bay seasoning

Pinch of salt

1 ½ cups of long-grain white rice

DIRECTIONS:

1. Place the inner cooking pot into the rice cooker, turn on and press the white rice button. Add the sausage to the inner cooking pot, keep the lid open, and cook the sausage for 5 minutes, until brown, while stirring occasionally with a wooden spoon, allowing the sausage to cook in its own grease.
2. Add the chopped celery, onion, okra, and pepper to the inner cooking pot, stirring continuously, keep the lid open, and cook for 5 more minutes, until the vegetables are soft and begin to release their fragrance.
3. Add the shrimp, beef broth, tomatoes, dried sassafras, Old Bay seasoning, salt, and hot sauce to the inner cooking pot, stir with the wooden spoon, then close the lid and leave to cook at the white rice setting for approximately 10 minutes.
4. Make sure the mixture has reached a boil, stir briefly with a wooden spoon then close the lid. Cook for approximately 5 more minutes, or until shrimp and sausage are cooked through. Switch to keep warm mode and let simmer until serving.
5. Portion the cooked long-grain white rice into individual serving bowls, then ladle the gumbo on top. Serve while hot.

MACARONI AND CHEESE

Forget mac'and'cheese out of a box or the freezer section, laden with chemicals and so-called "cheese product" (whatever that is). This homemade macaroni and three-cheese recipe is decadent, creamy, all-natural goodness – and it's wonderfully simple to prepare entirely in your rice cooker. Feel free to substitute regular water for the chicken or vegetable broth, but I find that using the broth to cook the pasta makes the whole dish particularly savory and irresistible.

Preparation time: 10 minutes

Cooking time: 45 minutes

Yields: 4 to 6

INGREDIENTS:

2 cups of elbow macaroni

2 cups of chicken or vegetable broth

1 cup of heavy cream

¾ cup of grated sharp cheddar

¾ cup of grated mozzarella

1/3 cup of grated parmesan

2 tablespoons of butter

½ teaspoon of salt

½ teaspoon of ground white pepper

DIRECTIONS:

1. Place the inner cooking pot into the rice cooker and add the broth, salt, and macaroni. Turn on the rice cooker and press the white rice button. Stir to combine the ingredients, close the lid and cook for 30 minutes, at which point the pasta will be cooked and will have absorbed most of the water in the broth.
2. Switch to keep warm mode, open the lid, and add the cream, cheddar, mozzarella, parmesan, butter, and white pepper. Stir with a wooden spoon until all ingredients are evenly combined, then close the lid and cook on keep warm for another 10 minutes, to achieve a light golden-brown crust on top.
3. Portion into individual serving bowls and serve warm or hot, perhaps with a side of vegetables or a fresh salad.

CRAYFISH (CRAWFISH) ÉTOUFFEE

This famous Louisiana Creole dish takes its name from the French word for "smothered" – *étouffée* – thanks to the method of its cooking, which involves low heat for long periods of time. This makes the dish ideal to prepare in a rice-cooker that comes with a low heat option, such as a "keep warm" setting. The centerpiece of this delicious dish is, of course, the crayfish – pronounced "crawfish," if you're local to Louisiana. Wherever you're from and whatever you call it, this étouffée is a true feast, sure to delight your friends, family, and guests.

Preparation time: 25 minutes

Cooking time: 1 hour 20 minutes

Yields: 4

INGREDIENTS:

3 cups of crawfish tails, peeled

¼ cup of clarified butter

¼ cup of all-purpose flour, sifted to remove lumps

½ cup of green onions (or scallions), rinsed and diced

1 large green bell pepper, rinsed, seeded and diced

3 large stalks of celery, rinsed and diced

3 teaspoons of ground dried paprika

1 ½ teaspoons of salt

1 teaspoon of garlic powder

1 teaspoon of ground black pepper

1 teaspoon of dried onion powder

1 teaspoon of dried ground cayenne pepper

1 teaspoon of dried ground oregano

1 teaspoon of dried ground thyme

1 ½ cups of cooked red rice

DIRECTIONS:

1. Place the inner cooking pot into the rice cooker, turn on and press the white rice button. Add the butter and let melt, stirring gently with a wooden spoon.
2. Once the butter begins to bubble, whisk in the flour, gently beating by hand until the flour is evenly mixed in and beginning to dissolve as it cooks into the butter.
3. After approximately 5 minutes, swap out the whisk for a wooden spoon, and continue to stir continuously until the mixture – now known as *roux* – has darkened to a light golden-brown color and has begun to release a nutty aroma.
4. Switch the rice cooker to keep warm mode, and continue to stir with the wooden spoon while adding the crayfish, green onions, bell pepper, paprika, salt, garlic powder, black pepper, onion powder, cayenne pepper, oregano, thyme, and chopped celery.
5. When all ingredients are evenly combined, close the lid and cook on keep warm mode for 1 hour.
6. Portion the cooked red rice into individual serving bowls, then ladle the étouffée on top. Serve while hot, perhaps with some extra chopped scallions sprinkled on top as a garnish. Portion into individual serving dishes and serve immediately.

WHOLE 'ROAST' CHICKEN

Ok, technically this isn't a real "roast" chicken because there is no flame. But it really doesn't matter, because once you taste chicken that's been cooked whole in the rice cooker, simmering in its own juices, butter, and a few key seasonings, you may never go back to the roasting pan again. This chicken makes a fantastic centerpiece for any hot meal, and it couldn't be easier.

Preparation time: 10 minutes

Cooking time: 45 minutes

Yields: 4

INGREDIENTS:

1 small whole chicken, 2 pounds

2 medium-sized white onions, peeled and cut in half

1 small lemon, cut into quarters, with seeds removed

3 sprigs of rosemary

2 tablespoons of butter, softened

Pinch of salt and pepper to taste

DIRECTIONS:

1. Place the four onion halves flat-side-down inside the inner cooking pot of the rice cooker.
2. Stuff the lemon wedges and the rosemary sprigs inside the whole chicken, then coat the chicken thoroughly with the softened butter, working it all around and even under the chicken skin. Sprinkle salt and pepper over the coated chicken.
3. Place the stuffed, seasoned and coated chicken inside the inner cooking pot, resting on the onion halves, and place the inner cooking pot into the rice cooker. Turn on the rice cooker and

press the white rice button. Cook for 1 hour or until chicken is cooked through, resetting to the white rice setting as needed.

4. Once chicken is cooked, either serve directly while hot or maintain in keep warm mode for up to two hours, then either serve or refrigerate. Portion the chicken onto plates along with the onion, and the starch dish of your choice, and consider garnishing with additional sprigs of rosemary and lemon wedges.

Steamed Tofu and Asparagus

This simple vegetarian dish is an excellent go-to hot meal for lunch or dinner, and it's hearty, filling and delicious enough that it's sure to satisfy meat-eaters and herbivores alike. This recipe uses just a touch of mirin, a type of rice wine available at most large grocery stores, but don't worry…the alcohol cooks off in the rice cooker, making this wholesome goodness perfectly suitable for children.

Preparation time: 5 minutes

Cooking time: 20 minutes

Yields: 4

INGREDIENTS:

1 bunch (approximately 6 ounces) of baby asparagus, rinsed, with the ends trimmed off and discarded

6 ounces of fried tofu, cut into bite-sized cubes

1 cup of filtered water, for steaming

1 small carrot, peeled and sliced into thin rounds

1 large clove of garlic, peeled and finely minced

2 tablespoons of soy sauce

1 teaspoon of vegetable oil

1 teaspoon of sesame oil

1 teaspoon of mirin rice wine

1 teaspoon of honey

1 ½ cups of cooked brown rice

DIRECTIONS:

1. Fill the inner cooking pot with 1 cup of water and place it in the rice cooker.
2. Place the cubed tofu and baby asparagus on the steam tray and place the steam tray into the inner cooking pot. Close the lid, turn on and press the steam button.
3. Let steam for 10 minutes, then lift lid and remove the steam tray and inner cooking pot. Discard the water from the inner cooking pot, and transfer the steamed tofu and asparagus from the steam tray into the inner cooking pot.
4. Place the inner cooking pot back inside the rice cooker, and add the thinly sliced carrot, the minced garlic, the soy sauce, the vegetable and sesame oils, the rice wine, and the honey.
5. Stir thoroughly with a wooden spoon until all ingredients are evenly blended, then close the lid and press the white rice button. Cook for another 10 minutes, or until the carrot slices have softened and the garlic and sesame oil have become fragrant.
6. Portion the cooked brown rice into individual serving bowls, then spoon the tofu, vegetables and sauce on top. Serve while hot, with extra soy sauce on the side for those who want it.

BLACK BEAN TACO SOUP

There are plenty of variations on taco soup, a classic of the American Southwest. My preferred rendition is this vegetarian recipe, which uses rich hearty black beans, a healthy dose of fresh vegetables, and fresh cilantro and chili peppers in the seasoning mix. This soup is a complete meal in itself, the perfect feast when you want a nutritious and filling meal.

Preparation time: 5 minutes

Cooking time: 40 minutes

Yields: 4

INGREDIENTS:

1 cup of black beans, rinsed and soaked, drained

3 cups of vegetable broth

¾ cup of loose sweetcorn, rinsed

1 large ripe tomato, rinsed and chopped

1 medium-sized white onion, peeled and chopped

2 large stalks of celery, rinsed and chopped

1 large green chili pepper, rinsed, seeded and chopped

¼ cup of fresh cilantro, rinsed and patted dry, finely minced

1 teaspoon of salt

1 teaspoon of ground black pepper

1 teaspoon of garlic powder

Corn tortilla chips, for serving

Sliced fresh avocado, for serving (optional)

Grated cheddar cheese or sour cream, for serving (optional)

DIRECTIONS:

1. Fill the inner cooking pot with the vegetable broth and place it in the rice cooker. Turn on the rice cooker and press the white rice button to heat the broth.
2. Add the beans, sweetcorn, tomato, onion, celery, chili pepper, cilantro, salt, black pepper, and garlic powder. Stir thoroughly with a long wooden spoon, until all ingredients are evenly mixed, then close the lid and let cook for 20 minutes.
3. After 20 minutes, open the lid and stir again with the wooden spoon. Switch the rice cooker setting to keep warm, and let simmer for another 20 minutes with the lid open, stirring occasionally with the wooden spoon. When done, the beans, celery and onions should all be softened and the soup releasing a savory aroma.
4. Portion the cooked soup into individual serving bowls, with tortilla chips on the side or crumbled on top. Add on any desired topping options, such as sliced avocado, sour cream or cheddar cheese, and serve while hot.

STEAMED HAWAIIAN MAHI MAHI

I've never actually been to Hawaii, but I've long been a fan of the mahi mahi fish found in its waters. The best part about this recipe – which I developed specifically for my rice-cooker and its handy-dandy steam tray – is the way the seasoned fish infuses and flavors the rice as it steams. This is an elegant and healthy meal for any time of year, as long as you can get your hands on the fish, so get ready for a gastronomic trip to the tropics!

Preparation time: 10 minutes

Cooking time: 25-30 minutes

Yields: 2

INGREDIENTS:

2 large mahi mahi filets, approximately 6 ounces each

1 cup of Basmati rice or any long-grain rice, rinsed and drained

Water, as needed to fill up to line 1

Salt, to taste (optional)

Marinade

2 tablespoons of soy sauce

2 tablespoons of toasted sesame oil

1 tablespoon of fresh ginger, finely minced

1 tablespoon of chopped green onions (scallions), for garnish

DIRECTIONS:

1. Take 1 cup of rice and place it in a fine strainer. Rinse with cool running water and drain thoroughly. Transfer rice to the inner cooking pot.
2. Fill the inner cooking pot with water up to line 1, or just above. Place the inner cooking pot into the rice cooker, swirl to combine and close the lid. Turn on and press the white rice button. Cook for 20 minutes.
3. While rice is cooking, in a separate mixing bowl whisk together the soy sauce, sesame oil, and minced ginger, stirring until evenly combined. Submerge the mahi mahi filets in the mixture, coating thoroughly on all sides, and leave to absorb the marinade for 10-20 minutes.
4. After 20 minutes, switch the rice cooker setting to steam. Lay the marinated mahi mahi filets on the steam tray, and place the steam tray on top of the inner cooking pot. Close the lid, turn on and press the steam button.
5. Let steam for 5-10 minutes, until the fish is cooked through and breaks apart easily with a wooden spoon, then remove the steam tray and inner cooking pot. Portion the rice equally onto serving plates, and lay the mahi mahi filets over the top. Garnish with the freshly chopped green onions.

DUCK BREAST WITH FINGERLING POTATOES

If you see a good cut of duck at the market, this recipe is a must-try. There really is very little in this world as sumptuous as crispy fingerling potatoes, infused with the aromas of seasoned duck cooking right in the same pot. That, in a nutshell, is what this dish offers, and it is simply sublime. With just a few herbs, seasonings, and the help of your trusty rice-cooker, prepare to enjoy a meal fit for a king.

Preparation time: 10 minutes

Cooking time: 35-40 minutes

Yields: 2

INGREDIENTS:

2 medium-sized duck breasts, skin on, approximately 6 ounces each

4 medium-sized fingerling potatoes, skin on, rinsed and sliced into bite-sized rounds

1 medium-sized carrot, peeled, rinsed and diced

1 tablespoon of extra virgin olive oil

1 teaspoon of salt

1 teaspoon of ground black pepper

2 tablespoons of butter, softened

1 teaspoon of dried ground rosemary

1 pinch of kosher salt

2 large cloves of garlic, peeled and finely minced

DIRECTIONS:

1. Place the olive oil, salt, pepper, carrots, and fingerling potatoes inside the inner cooking pot, and use a wooden spoon to stir gently, ensuring that the potatoes and carrots are evenly and thoroughly coated with oil and seasonings. Place the inner cooking pot into the rice cooker, set the white rice button, and leave the lid open to begin cooking.
2. In a mixing bowl, combine the softened butter with the ground rosemary, kosher salt, and minced garlic, ensuring that all ingredients are evenly blended. Rub the mixture thoroughly over all sides of the duck breasts, even working it underneath the skin.
3. Place the coated and seasoned duck breasts in the steam tray, and place the steam tray on top of the carrots and potatoes in the inner cooking pot. Turn on and set the white rice button. Cook for 20 minutes.
4. After 20 minutes, open the lid and, using tongs and a wooden spoon, turn over the duck breasts and gently stir the potatoes and carrots, to ensure even cooking. Close the lid, turn on and press white rice button.
5. Cook for another 15 minutes, or when duck is cooked through and the potatoes are crisped to a golden brown. Remove the steam tray and inner cooking pot. Portion the potatoes, carrots and duck equally onto serving plates and serve immediately while hot.

MUSSELS IN WHITE WINE AND SAFFRON BROTH

Steamed mussels are a summertime tradition in my family, and my absolute favorite preparation is this awesome recipe that I adapted for my rice cooker. The delicate flavor combination of the shallots, parsley and garlic mingling with the saffron and white wine in the broth is simply divine – and the perfect infusion for the steaming mussels and tomatoes. This is a wonderful warm-weather dish to share for an elegant meal, paired with a crisp glass of dry white wine for the adults.

Preparation time: 5 minutes

Cooking time: 10-15 minutes

Yields: 2

INGREDIENTS:

1.5 pounds of fresh mussels

15 threads of saffron

1/3 cup of dry white wine

1 tablespoon of unsalted butter, softened

1 large shallot, thinly sliced

1 large clove of garlic, peeled and finely minced

½ teaspoon of salt

½ teaspoon of ground black pepper

1 large ripe tomato, rinsed and coarsely chopped

1 tablespoon of fresh flat-leaf parsley, rinsed and patted dry, coarsely chopped

2 thick slices of crusty bread or baguette, for serving

DIRECTIONS:

1. Add 2 cups of water to the inner cooking pot. Place the mussels on the steam tray, put the steam tray into the inner pot and secure the lid. Press the steam button and steam for 6-8 minutes. Check to make sure mussels have opened. When opened, remove the steam tray and cover the mussels to keep them warm. Dump the water from the inner pot and wipe clean.
2. Place the saffron, white wine, butter, shallot, garlic, salt, pepper, tomato, and parsley all together inside the inner cooking pot. Place the inner cooking pot into the rice cooker, set to white rice, and leave the lid open to begin cooking.
3. With a long wooden spoon, stir gently, combining the ingredients. After 5 minutes, the butter should be melted and the ingredients thoroughly mixed. Add the mussels to the inner cooking pot, stir gently for another 1-2 minutes with the lid still open.
4. Portion the mussels with the broth and tomatoes into serving bowls. Serve immediately while hot, with the side of crusty bread to help absorb the broth.

GARLIC BUTTERED LOBSTER RICE

Get ready for a seriously decadent meal – perfect for special occasions and intimate celebrations. This lobster and rice dish is as deceptively simple as it is irresistible. If you've never before tasted rice steamed in butter, garlic and lobster aromas, be prepared for a taste revelation. And that's all before we get to the actual lobster, whose luxurious meat comes out so tender, so succulent and juicy when prepared in the rice cooker, that I predict you'll abandon your stovetop lobster pot for good!

Preparation time: 10 minutes

Cooking time: 25-30 minutes

Yields: 2

INGREDIENTS:

2 medium-sized lobster tails, approximately 6 ounces each, shell-on.

1 cup of Basmati rice or any long-grain rice, rinsed and drained

Water, as needed to fill up to line 1

Salt, to taste (optional)

2 tablespoons of clarified butter, softened

3 large cloves of garlic, peeled and finely minced

1 teaspoon of kosher salt

½ teaspoon of ground black pepper

1 tablespoon of fresh chives, rinsed and patted dry, coarsely chopped

Lemon wedges for garnish

DIRECTIONS:

1. Take 1 cup of rice and place it in a fine strainer. Rinse with cool running water and drain thoroughly. Transfer rice to the inner cooking pot.
2. Fill the inner cooking pot with water up to line 1, or just above. Place the inner cooking pot into the rice cooker, swirl to combine and close the lid. Turn on and press the white rice button. Cook for 15 minutes.
3. While rice is cooking, in a separate mixing bowl mix together the softened butter, minced garlic, chopped chives, salt, and pepper. Stir until all ingredients are thoroughly mixed. Spread the butter mixture thoroughly over the lobster tails, working it down between the shell and the meat, coating completely.
4. After 15 minutes, switch the rice cooker setting to steam. Lay the coated lobster tails, shell-side down, on the steam tray, and place the steam tray into the inner cooking pot. Close the lid, turn on and press the steam button.
5. Let steam for 12-15 minutes, until the lobster is cooked through and breaks away easily from the shell when nudged with a wooden spoon. Remove the steam tray and inner cooking pot. Portion the rice onto serving plates, and lay the lobster tails over the top, either still in the shell or removed with the meat sliced. Garnish with the lemon wedges, and serve while hot.

QUINOA POMEGRANATE SALAD

Many are intimidated by quinoa since it's so tricky to prepare on the stovetop – which is a shame, because this whole grain seed is packed with protein and makes for an incredibly healthy meal. Thankfully, a good rice cooker makes perfectly cooked quinoa a total snap, and from there, it's just a matter of letting it cool down, mixing in luscious ruby-red pomegranate seeds and a few other seasonings to complement the quinoa's woody flavors, and you've got yourself a nutritious, delicious, and beautiful dish!

Preparation time: 2 hours

Cooking time: 30 minutes

Yields: 4

INGREDIENTS:

2 cups of quinoa, rinsed and strained

Vegetable stock, as needed to fill up to line 3

1 teaspoon of table salt

1 cup of fresh pomegranate seeds, rinsed and drained

2 tablespoons of toasted pine nuts

½ teaspoon of allspice powder

½ cup of fresh mint, rinsed and patted dry, finely chopped

1 tablespoon of olive oil

½ teaspoon of coarsely ground sea salt

½ teaspoon of ground black pepper

1 teaspoon of lemon juice

DIRECTIONS:

1. Add rinsed and drained quinoa and the table salt to the inner cooking pot. Fill the inner cooking pot with vegetable broth up to line 3. Place the inner cooking pot into the rice cooker, swirl to combine and close the lid securely.
2. Turn on the rice cooker, and press the white rice button to start cooking. Let cook for 30 minutes.
3. When the quinoa is done, lift the lid and fluff the quinoa.
4. Transfer to a large mixing bowl, cover and leave to cool for at least 1 hour. Remember to refrigerate the quinoa after no more than 2 hours, since it should not sit at room temperature longer than 120 minutes.
5. Once the cooked quinoa has cooled, add the pomegranate seeds, pine nuts, allspice, mint, olive oil, sea salt, pepper, and lemon juice to the mixing bowl. Using a large wooden spoon, gently but thoroughly fold the ingredients, stirring until all ingredients are evenly mixed.
6. Either serve directly by portioning out the quinoa salad into serving bowls, or cover the mixing bowl and refrigerate until ready for serving. Can be served warm or chilled.

STEAMED LITTLENECK CLAMS IN BEER BROTH

This all-American dish of littleneck clams steamed in a buttery, garlicky beer broth is the perfect light but festive meal for the height of summer. The alcohol in the beer cooks off in the rice cooker, meaning this dish is perfectly "Safe" for children and non-drinkers, but not before it infuses the clams with an aromatic earthy flavor that jives perfectly with the garlic, lemon, and seasonings in this simple yet sophisticated dish.

Preparation time: 5 minutes

Cooking time: 20-25 minutes

Yields: 2

INGREDIENTS:

2 pounds of littleneck clams

12-ounce bottle of beer, preferably a light wheat ale

2 large cloves of garlic, peeled and finely minced

½ a medium-sized lemon, seeds removed, sliced into wedges

2 tablespoons of butter, softened

1 tablespoon of Old Bay Seasoning

1 teaspoon of salt

1 teaspoon of ground black pepper

Two thick slices of crusty bread, for serving

DIRECTIONS:

1. Pour the beer into the inner cooking pot, and add the minced garlic, the lemon wedges, softened butter, Old Bay seasoning, salt, and pepper. Place the inner cooking pot into the rice cooker, set to white rice, and leave the lid open to begin cooking.
2. With a long wooden spoon, stir gently, combining the ingredients. After 6-7 minutes, the butter should be melted, the ingredients thoroughly mixed, and the mixture simmering at a low boil.
3. Add the clams to the inner cooking pot, keep the rice cooker on the white rice setting, and close the lid. Cook with the lid closed on white rice mode for 5 minutes, then switch the rice cooker to steam and keep the lid closed.
4. Let steam for 6-8 minutes, or until clams are cooked through and the shells have opened wide, then open the lid and remove the inner cooking pot. Portion the clams with the broth equally in serving bowls. Serve immediately while hot, with the side of crusty bread to help absorb the broth.

PHILLY CHEESESTEAKS

Think you need to travel to Philadelphia to get that amazing classic cheesesteak taste? Think again! This recipe gets the traditional ooey-gooey cheesy steak sandwich flavors just right, and it couldn't be easier to prepare at home in your rice cooker. Get ready for the ultimate sandwich satisfaction!

Preparation time: 20 minutes

Cooking time: 2 to 3 hours

Yields: 4

INGREDIENTS:

1 large onion, halved crosswise and thinly sliced

1 large bell peppers, halved lengthwise and thinly sliced

2 cups of beef top sirloin steak, thinly sliced into strips

1 package of onion soup mix

2 cups of beef stock

4 hoagie buns, sliced in the middle

8 slices of provolone cheese

Pickled spiced cherry peppers, chopped

DIRECTIONS:

1. Place the inner cooking pot into the rice cooker, add the onion, bell pepper, beef, onion soup mix and pour in the stock. Stir to combine, close the lid and cook for about 1 hour or until the rice cooker switches to keep warm mode.
4. Reset the rice cooker to cook for another cooking interval. Cook for another hour then maintain cooking in keep warm mode.

When the beef is very tender, prepare the buns and other ingredients.

5. Split the buns and add the cheese on one side, top with beef slices, onions and peppers. Add a layer of cherry peppers. Serve immediately.

SLOPPY JOES

My family are all huge sloppy joe fans, and there's nothing I love more than to prepare them fresh right in my own kitchen. This recipe uses a touch of pickle relish for just the right seasoning blend, and the celery and onion in the mix help keep the beef fresh and juicy for every bite.

Preparation time: 10 minutes

Cooking time: 2 hours

Yields: 6

INGREDIENTS:

1 pound of lean beef, ground

1 medium stalk of celery, diced

1 medium onion, diced

1 cup chili sauce

1 ½ tablespoons of sugar

2 teaspoons sweet pickle relish

2 teaspoon of Worcestershire sauce

½ teaspoon table salt

¼ teaspoon of crushed black pepper

6 burger buns, split

DIRECTIONS:

1. Place the inner cooking pot into the rice cooker and add the ground beef, celery and onions. Turn on the rice cooker and press the white rice button, close the lid and cook until the meat is no longer pink while stirring occasionally.

2. Drain excess fat and stir in the sugar, chili sauce, pickle relish, Worcestershire sauce and season with salt and pepper. Close the lid and cook for 1 hour or until the rice cooker switches to keep warm mode. Maintain in keep warm mode for 30 minutes and remove the inner cooking pot from the rice cooker.
3. Add ½ cup of meat mixture on top of each bun and serve.

Pulled Pork

My whole family has a serious weakness for pulled pork – tender, juicy, lightly seasoned and oh-so-delicious in sandwiches or atop veggies and rice; we just can't get enough. This recipe is my go-to preparation, and it's never let me down. I know it'll work up a treat in your kitchen as well.

Preparation time: 5 minutes

Cooking time: 2 hours

Yields: 6

INGREDIENTS:

1 ½ pound of pork loin, excess fat trimmed

1 ½ cups stock or broth

1 ½ cups of water

1 cup of any barbecue sauce

1 teaspoon crushed black pepper

1 teaspoon of salt

DIRECTIONS:

1. Add all ingredients except for the meat into the inner cooking pot, stir to combine and place the inner cooking pot into the rice cooker. Add the meat, turn on the rice cooker and press the white rice button. Close the lid and cook for about 2 hours or until the meat is fork tender.
2. If the rice cooker switched to keep warm mode and is not yet done, reset and cook until the meat is tender. After the rice cooker has switched to keep warm mode for the second time, it should bc donc.
3. Transfer the meat into a large bowl to cool, then shred it with two forks and serve with buns or bread.

Sweet 'n' Tangy Chicken Wings

This recipe creates classic sweet and tangy "barbecued" chicken wings – without actually having to drag out your barbecue! These wings couldn't be simpler with a good rice cooker, and they taste like tender, succulent, juicy heaven. This is a perfect option to serve on game days or family events, for a meal that is literally finger-licking good!

Preparation time: 20 minutes

Cooking time: 2 hours

Yields: 6 to 8

INGREDIENTS:

1 pound chicken wings

½ teaspoon of salt, divided

½ teaspoon crushed pepper

1 cup of ketchup

4 tablespoon of brown sugar

4 tablespoons of red wine vinegar

1 tablespoon of Worcestershire sauce

2 teaspoon of Dijon mustard

1 garlic clove, minced

1 teaspoon of toasted sesame seeds, optional

DIRECTIONS:

1. Season the chicken with salt and crushed pepper and add into the inner cooking pot. Place the inner cooking pot into the rice cooker, turn on and press the white rice button. Brown the

chicken on all sides. Ina small bowl, combine the remaining ingredients, except for the sesame seeds and pour over the chicken wings.

2. Stir the ingredients until chicken is well coated, close the lid and cook for 1 hour or until the chicken is cooked through. Stir the ingredients well and cook until the sauce has thickened to taste.
3. Sprinkle with toasted sesame seeds and toss to combine. Switch to keep warm mode and let it cook with low heat before serving.
4. Transfer to a serving dish and serve immediately.

10

DESSERT

RICE PUDDING, INDIAN STYLE

This Indian-style rice pudding, flavored with cardamom and a base of long-grain or basmati rice, is a wonderfully exotic take on the standard rice pudding. I particularly love the slivered almonds in this preparation, which give every bite a terrific nutty touch. This dessert is a huge hit at my house, and I know your friends, family and guests will adore it as well.

Preparation time: 5 minutes

Cooking time: 1 hour to 1 hour 30 minutes

Yields: 3 to 4

INGREDIENTS:

½ cup of Basmati rice or any long-grain rice, rinsed and drained

3 cup of milk, or as needed

½ cup packed sugar, or as needed according to taste

2 tablespoons slivered almonds

1 cardamom pod

DIRECTIONS:

1. Place all ingredients into the inner cooking pot and stir to combine. Transfer the inner cooking pot into the rice cooker, turn on and press the white rice button to start cooking. Close the lid and cook for about 1 hour or until it switches to keep warm mode. Open the lid after the first 30 minutes of cooking to avoid over spilling of the inner pot contents and check regularly.

5. When the mixture has thickened and the rice has softened, switch to keep warm mode and let it stand for 10 minutes. You can add more milk and adjust the taste by adding more milk and sugar until the desired consistency and taste is achieved.

Tatin Cake

This delicate little dessert is the French twist on apple pie, and it's truly a sophisticated dish to serve up at the end of a tea or dinner party. Your guests will think you've spent hours slaving over your gourmet French culinary skills – so no need to tell them how easy this delicacy was achieved in your rice cooker!

Preparation time: 15 minutes

Cooking time: 45 minutes

Yields: 3 to 4

INGREDIENTS:

2 apples, cored and sliced into wedges

2 tablespoons butter

3 tablespoons brown sugar

½ cup flour, sifted

¼ cup white sugar

½ teaspoon of baking powder

Pinch of salt

3 tablespoons of butter, melted

2 medium whole eggs

DIRECTIONS:

1. Combine together the flour, white sugar, baking powder and salt in a mixing bowl and mix in 3 tablespoons of melted butter and the eggs. Mix it thoroughly until well combined and set aside.
2. Place the inner cooking pot into the rice cooker, turn the rice cooker on and press the white rice button to melt the 2 tablespoons of butter.

3. Once the butter has melted, add the apples and cook for 5 minutes while tossing frequently to cook them evenly. Stir in the brown sugar and cook until the sugar starts to caramelize.
4. Arrange the apple wedges on the bottom of the pan and add in the batter mixture on top. With a serving spatula, even out the dough and cover the apples completely.
5. Close the lid and cook for about 20 to 25 minutes or until done. It is done when a toothpick inserted into the thickest part comes out clean. Switch to keep warm mode and let it stand for 10 minutes.
6. Carefully flip the inner cooking pot upside down onto a serving dish, releasing the cake. Serve immediately.

Banana Pudding with Caramel Sauce

I love a good banana and caramel pudding, but until recently I never seemed to have time to prepare it at home. That's until I learned this terrific recipe to make it using my rice cooker. Now, this old favorite makes a regular appearance at my dining table, to the cheers of my family – and best of all, it's a breeze to put together!

Preparation time: 15 minutes

Cooking time: 45 to 50 minutes

Yields: 4

INGREDIENTS:

Banana Pudding

6 tablespoons unsalted melted butter, divided

5 tablespoons packed brown sugar, divided

1 ripe banana, peeled sliced into rounds

2 ripe bananas, peeled and mashed

1 medium whole egg, beaten

2 small pinches or ½ teaspoon of cinnamon spice powder

2 to 3 tablespoons of milk

1 cup of sifted self-rising flour

Caramel sauce, for serving

DIRECTIONS:

1. Combine together 4 tablespoons of melted butter, egg, 3 tablespoons of brown sugar, cinnamon, mashed banana and milk in a large mixing bowl. Mix it thoroughly until well combined.

Mix in the flour into the banana mixture and stir again until well incorporated. Set aside.

2. Lightly grease the inner cooking pot with oil and line with parchment paper. Pour in 2 tablespoons of melted butter and sprinkle 2 tablespoons of brown sugar evenly in the inner pot. Place a layer of the sliced ripe bananas over the butter and sugar mixture.
3. Add the flour and mashed banana mixture into the inner cooking pot and spread with the serving spatula until evenly distributed.
4. Turn on the rice cooker and press the white rice button. Close the lid and cook for about 20 to 25 minutes or until the top part is done. It is done when a toothpick inserted into the thickest part comes out clean. When it is done, switch to keep warm mode and let it stand for 10 minutes before serving.
5. Carefully flip the inner cooking pot upside down onto a serving plate to release the pudding and serve immediately with caramel sauce on top.

CHOCOLATE STEEL CUT OATS

Fans of nutritious steel-cut oats really get their taste for good health rewarded with this wonderfully innovative dessert. The cocoa powder, chocolate chips, and the touch of sugar in this recipe are all it takes to turn wholesome oats into a sumptuous and irresistible dessert. Whip up a batch today, and enjoy a sweet dish that's both nutritious and delicious!

Preparation time: 5 minutes

Cooking time: 1 hour to 1 hour 30 minutes

Yields: 4

INGREDIENTS:

1 cup steel cut oats

2 cups water

1 cup of milk

1 tablespoon cocoa powder

2 tablespoons of sugar, or as needed according to taste

2 tablespoons of chocolate chips, for serving

DIRECTIONS:

1. Place the inner cooking pot into the rice cooker and add all ingredients except for the chocolate chips. Stir the ingredients, turn on the rice cooker and press the white rice button to start cooking. Close the lid and cook for about 1 hour or until the oats are soft and the consistency has thickened.
2. Switch to keep warm mode and let it stand for 10 minutes. You can also add more milk and sugar until preferred consistency or taste is achieved.
3. Portion cooked chocolate oats into individual serving bowls and serve warm with chocolate chips on top.

Poached Pears in Pomegranate

This sweetly flavored dessert is a truly gourmet way to present a delicious and beautiful dish. The combination of tart, juicy pomegranate with the gentle sweetness of pears is really irresistible, making this the perfect dessert to serve after a dinner party any time of year.

Preparation time: 5 minutes

Cooking time: 2 hours

Yields: 4

INGREDIENTS:

2 firm ripe and slim pears, core and peeled, cut into half

1 ½ to 2 cups of pomegranate juice

1 cup apple cider

1 cup apple juice

3-inch stick of cinnamon

1 clove

1 star anise

1 cardamom pod

1-inch piece of fresh ginger root, grated

DIRECTIONS:

1. Place the inner cooking pot into the rice cooker and add in the juices, apple cider, cinnamon, star anise, clove, cardamom and ginger. Stir the ingredients well and add the pear halves into the inner cooking pot. Close the lid, turn on the rice cooker and press the white rice button. Cook pears for about 50 minutes, or until the pears are tender.

2. Switch to keep warm mode and turn the pears over to cook and coat the other side with the poaching liquid. Close the lid and let it stand for an hour.
3. Remove the pears carefully from the inner cooking pot and serve warm or chilled.

CHOCOLATE LAVA CAKE

Everyone loves a good deep, dark, hot-in-the-center chocolate cake – and this lava cake is as good as it comes. A good rice-cooker makes this decadent dessert wonderfully easy to prepare, and perfect to impress the chocolate lovers in your life.

Preparation time: 15 minutes

Cooking time: 1 hour to 1 hour 30 minutes

Yields: 4 to 6

INGREDIENTS:

1 package or box of chocolate moist cake mix

Other ingredients needed to prepare the cake mix

1 can (16 oz) of milk chocolate frosting, divided

Oil, for greasing

DIRECTIONS:

1. Place the half of the chocolate frosting mixture in small bowl and chill 1 hour before cooking.
2. Combine together all ingredients for the chocolate cake in a mixing bowl and mix until well incorporated.
3. Lightly grease the inner cooking pot with oil and place into the rice cooker. Pour in half of the cake batter and add the chilled chocolate frosting on the center. Pour in the remaining cake batter and close the lid securely. Turn on the rice cooker and press the white rice button to start cooking.
4. Cook for 25 to 30 minutes or until the batter on the top part is almost done. Close the lid and switch to keep warm mode. Cook for another 30 minutes until the cake is done.

5. It is done when a toothpick inserted on the part where there is no chocolate frosting comes out clean.
6. When the cake is done, gently flip the inner cooking pot upside down onto a serving plate. You may need to run a dull knife along the edge to loosen. Set aside and let it rest.
7. Return the inner cooking pot into the rice cooker and press the white rice button. Pour in the reserved chocolate frosting and cook until warmed through.
8. Pour the chocolate frosting over the cake and serve immediately.

Almond Cream Coconut Flan

By the end of the day, I never seem to have time to cook dessert. Thankfully, having the rice cooker has made it easy to pull together something to satisfy my family's sweet tooth. One taste of this awesome almond-cream coconut-infused dessert, creamy as can be and uniquely delicious, and your family will grateful you made the time to make this for them.

Preparation time: 10 minutes

Cooking time: 1 hour

Yields: 6

INGREDIENTS:

2 cups of water, for steaming

4 egg yolks

¼ cup of sugar, divided

A pinch of salt

2 cups of heavy cream, divided

½ tablespoon of almond extract

½ cup of shredded coconut

DIRECTIONS:

1. Place the inner cooking pot into the rice cooker and add half the cream, half the sugar, shredded coconut and almond extract. Transfer the inner cooking pot into the rice cooker, turn on and press the white rice button. Cook the mixture for 5 minutes or until it starts to form bubbles while stirring regularly. Transfer into a bowl and let it rest to cool.
2. Return the inner cooking pot into the rice cooker, pour in 2 cups of water and press the power button. Close the lid, press the white rice or steam button and bring the water to a boil.

3. Whisk together half the cream, yolks, salt and half of the sugar in a mixing bowl until well combined.
4. Gradually add in the cooked cream mixture while whisking constantly until well incorporated. Pour it all into a baking dish that is a size that fits into the inner cooking pot and steam tray. Cover the baking dish with aluminum foil and crimp the edges to seal. Place the baking dish on the steam tray.
5. Carefully open the lid of the rice cooker place the steam tray with the baking dish on it into the inner cooking pot. Close the lid and cook for about 50 minutes.
6. When the almond coconut cream is done, carefully remove the steam tray with a mitt and let the coconut flan rest for 10 minutes without the foil.
7. Serve almond coconut cream flan chilled or immediately after resting.

COCONUT BLACK RICE PUDDING

This black rice pudding infused with sweet coconut and a touch of brown sugar is an amazing dessert to serve when you really want to delight your guests' palates. It's surprisingly easy to prepare – though no need to tell your diners that. Best to just let them imagine it took you hours of work for this incredible result.

Preparation time: 5 minutes

Cooking time: 1 hour, 10 minutes

Yields: 3 to 4

INGREDIENTS:

1 cup of black glutinous rice, soaked for 2 hours and drained

3 cups of water

½ cup of brown sugar

1 cup canned coconut cream, for serving

DIRECTIONS:

1. Place the rice and water in the inner cooking pot, turn the rice cooker on and press the white rice button to start cooking. Close the lid and cook for about 1 hour until the rice is soft and tender and the consistency is thick. You may add more water to adjust consistency if desired. Reset the rice cooker and manually switch to keep warm mode when done.
2. Add the sugar and switch to keep warm mode, stir and let it stand for 10 minutes until or until the sugar is completely dissolved.
3. Portion black rice pudding into individual serving bowls and drizzle with coconut cream on top. Serve warm.

Creamy Coconut Fruit and Root Veggies

This dish is one of my all-time favorites to serve as a pudding, or even a snack on special occasions. The coconut, tapioca and root vegetables marry for a flavor sensation, and a taste that is as unique as it is delicious. Enjoy!

Preparation time: 20 minutes

Cooking time: 1 hour

Yields: 6 to 8

INGREDIENTS:

½ cup of diced sweet potatoes

½ cup of diced purple yam

½ cup of diced plantains

½ cup of ripe jackfruit, sliced into long strips

½ cup of cooked small tapioca pearls

½ cup of granulated sugar, or as needed to taste

1 cup coconut milk

1 cup water

DIRECTIONS:

1. Pour in the water and add the potatoes, yam, plantains and jackfruit in the inner cooking pot. Transfer the inner cooking into the rice cooker, turn on and press the white rice button. Close the lid and cook until the vegetables are almost tender, or for 30 minutes.

2. Stir in the coconut milk, sugar and the tapioca in the inner cooking pot and close the lid. Cook for another 20 minutes or until the ingredients are cooked through and tender and the consistency has thickened.

3. Switch to keep warm mode, adjust taste and consistency and let it stand for 10 minutes.
4. Portion dessert soup into individual serving bowls and serve warm or cool.

Cocoa Rice Pudding

I come from a long line of chocolate lovers, so this is my favorite of all the rice puddings out there. The rice pudding is made even creamier with the addition of the cocoa. I feel the brown sugar is the best sugar for the recipe, but use whatever you have on hand.

Preparation time: 5 minutes

Cooking time: 40 minutes

Yields: 4

INGREDIENTS:

½ cup of Arborio rice, rinsed and drained

2 cups of canned coconut milk

1 cup of water

¼ cup of unsweetened cocoa powder

½ cup raw cane or brown sugar

Evaporated milk, for serving

DIRECTIONS:

1. Place the rice and water into the inner cooking pot, turn on the rice cooker and press the white rice button. Close the lid and bring to a boil.
2. Add in the coconut milk, cocoa powder and sugar and close the lid. Cook for about 30 minutes or until the rice is soft and the consistency has thickened. Switch to keep warm mode and cook for 10 minutes more.
3. Portion pudding into individual serving bowls and drizzle with evaporated milk on top. Serve warm or cool.

DON'T FORGET!

For great deals and bargains on fun rice cooker related kitchenware, go to my website,

www.ContemporaryCupboard.com

And because you bought this book, you get a 15% discount! Simply use Coupon Code "bliss" at checkout.